COOKS, CLOWNS AND COWBOYS

101 SKILLS AND EXPERIENCES TO DISCOVER ON YOUR TRAVELS

lonely planet

Melbourne * London * Oakland

COOKS, CLOWNS AND COWBOYS

IT'S TIME TO LEARN SOMETHING NEW.

You know the feeling. One day you wake up and suddenly the job you do, the streets you know – they're no longer enough. It's time to get away, take on a challenge, try something you never imagined you would. **But what, where and when do you start?**

We know that feeling, too. That's why we started this book. Because sometimes it isn't enough just to go. You need to give yourself a reason.

At its heart, our desire to travel is about **fulfilling our human need to explore,** to meet new people and see the world through the lens of different cultures. By going out there beyond the horizon, immersing ourselves in strange new worlds, we know our lives will be changed forever.

Whether it's learning to **trek the snow-capped ledges in Nepal** or discovering the **secret to making perfect pizzas in Napoli,** what we learn our travels shines a light on what motivates us, the things we love, the things we cannot do without. In essence, travel helps teach us about who we really are.

So let **Cooks, Clowns and Cowboys** be your starting point. Let it tempt you with a reason to begin your next adventure.

Think of this book as an invitation to explore, and not just far-flung corners of the planet, but also your own infinite, inner potential.

And let these experiences serve as an icebreaker. Because, by challenging yourself with any or all of these **101 awesome activities,** you'll discover that taking part is the first step towards fitting in. Saying that you'll try something new, that you'll give it a go, is like making a peace offering to the locals. It's a sign of your natural curiosity and respect for their way of life and everything it might teach you.

Once that offer has been made and the ice is well and truly broken, it's time to follow your unique spirit of adventure. Let it be your guide. **Who knows where it will lead you?**

Showing off sublime flamenco moves in Seville.

COOKS, CLOWNS AND COWBOYS

A human being should be able to dance **the rumba,** lasso **a steer,** play **the sitar,** grow **their own food, mix a martini, centre their chakras, and** build **an igloo. "Specialisation is for insects."* Why not do them all and wear your 'badges' with pride...**

* With thanks, and apologies, to Robert Heinlein.

Music & Dance

Get set to unleash your inner luvvie and go break a leg. The activities you must complete to earn your Music and Dance badge concentrate on developing your sense of rhythm and shaking it like you just don't care. Preferably in public. You might find yourself in Cuban bars doing the rumba or taking centre stage masquerading as a Beijing opera star. Wherever your pursuit of this exquisite badge takes you, remember to limber up, feel the beat, and let your spirit move you.

Active

As well as taking you to some of the most spectacular landscapes, the Active badge will see you pushing your body to its limits. Not just physically, mentally, too. It takes nerves of steel, not to mention a low centre of gravity, to knock competitors' off their skates in a roller derby, and you'll discover that sledding across the Yukon is more about how well you can bond with a huskie than how tight you can grip the reins. Channelling your inner dude as you surf into another epic wave in Hawaii, you'll wonder how anyone could ever end up as a couch potato.

Culture & Language

Sure, most of us have culture and we can all speak a language but to earn this badge you'll need to feel a new vibe. This one is all about dancing to the beat of a different drum, learning the lingo of a foreign tongue, and loving it. You could be tripping out on voodoo in Ghana or thawing out in an igloo you just built yourself in Alaska. As you begin to appreciate the myriad small things that ensure no two cultures are the same, you'll be able to tell your new found friends, in their own language, that you are so glad you came.

Flora & Fauna

Greenies and anyone who loves getting stuck into mud will love what's needed to acquire this badge. You'll soon be getting your gorilla on in old-growth forests, then staying the urban sprawl across Cape Town, before tracking your own wolf pack across magnificent Euro mountains. By taking that moment to stop to smell the roses, or equivalent flower that's indigenous to the region, it becomes crystal clear how much we are all a product of our environment. Big respect to Mama Nature.

Food & Drink

This very popular badge is subject to misinterpretation. It is not just about sampling delectable dishes and getting ripped on rum. Like the Active badge, this one requires you to get involved. Don't just sip on a pisco sour, learn how to make one. To earn this badge, foodie 'bystanders' will need to step into the limelight and get a sweat on in the kitchen, behind the bar, or out in the markets. The proof of whether you've earned this badge will be in deliciousness of your pudding, pizza, handmade cheese, or whatever else piques your passion. Yum!

Mind & Body

This badge is perfect for stress heads as by the time you're ready to pin this one on your sleeves you'll be astrally projecting halfway to Nirvana, or at the very least you'll have learned how to relax. You may reckon it's easy to master the art of relaxation in a picturesque temple hidden in a far away jungle paradise, but tapping into inner peace might not be as intuitive as we think. If you're committed to earning your Mind & Body badge you'll need to pay close attention to your instructors, be they monk, masseuse or survival coach.

Art & Crafts

If you're good with your hands, this badge is for you, and a light, artistic touch will be handy if you opt for egg painting in the Ukraine or creating complex batik designs in Bali. But fear not, there is an Arts and Crafts activity to suit every taste. Even the most Philistine among us should be able to 'smashion' something from the blacksmith's hearth. Or if that sounds like too much sweat and tears, head to California and fashion a fiddle. The beauty of earning this badge is that you'll have something tangible to show off for it, forever

SADDLE UP WITH GAUCHOS IN ARGENTINA

Duration One day ✳ **Cost** US$102 ✳ **Outcome** A taste of Argentinean traditions, the thrill of the great outdoors, and some hands-on horse-handling skills ✳ **Where** Zárate, Argentina

How it suits you

This outdoor, horseback experience suits active animal-lovers who value the challenge of a one-on-one adventure. It also helps if you're spontaneous and up for just about anything. Those who can't or don't want to ride a pony can jump into a sulky – a traditional two-wheeled horse-drawn carriage.

What you'll get from it

★ **Insight** Gaucho Don Juan and charming hosts Ana and Pancho will tell you all about Argentinean rural traditions and welcome you into their large family, taking you right into the heart and soul of the country.

★ **Practical skills** Depending on the day, you might find yourself herding sheep or rounding up horses, in true gaucho style.

★ **Edible culture** Enjoy energising *yerba mate* tea, a hearty breakfast, appetisers of *empanadas* (mini pasties stuffed with meat, cheese or vegetables) and a belt-busting lunch of traditional *asado* (barbecue).

Practical details

Be a gaucho for the day with **Los Dos Hermanos** (estancialosdoshermanos.com), which can arrange transport from Buenos Aires. Overnight accommodation is offered in rustic cabins, so you can stay on to enjoy evening tales of gaucho bravado and songs around the fire under the stars.

Other options

A thriving gaucho culture is also alive and kicking in Brazil, where **Far and Ride** (farandride.com) runs riding holidays. And a cowboy-style experience in the US through **Equestrian Safaris** (safaririding.com) or in the UK through **Studland Stables** (studlandstables.com) would also help get you in the mood.

Doing it at home

Keep the gaucho traditions alive at home by drinking *yerba mate* tea from a gourd and *bombilla* (steel straw). Don the stylish gaucho uniform of beret, distinctive *bombachas* (pleated trousers), and flamboyant but functional *facón* (long knife).

WHAT TO EXPECT

Toss aside any notions of stiff riding schools, trotting around a paddock or dull instructions. Get ready to experience life on an authentic *estancia* (Argentinean ranch) with a genuine resident gaucho.

After saddling up your horse yourself (this is hands-on, remember), and

Unleash your inner cowboy in the wild open plains of the Pampas, home to Argentina's legendary, larger-than-life national icon, the gaucho.

holding your reins loosely, gaucho-style, it's time to walk or trot – gauchos don't gallop unless there is a real emergency – into the Pampas.

On the wide, open plains dotted with eucalyptus trees and crossed by small rivers, you will meet Tito the grumpy donkey, spot local birds and wildlife and get the chance to breathe in the great outdoors.

Don't expect to have your hands held and do be prepared to get your hands dirty, right down to washing down your trusty steed at the end of the day. Though every need is catered for, this is a welcome world away from the luxurious and often touristy ranches in the rest of the country. It's an experience that's not stage-managed, so the outcome very much depends on the day and what you encounter along the way ...

Gauchos of the Pampas ride locally bred Criollo horses.

POUND OUT A POTENT
CURRY IN CHIANG MAI

Duration One day ✳ **Cost** Around 1000 baht ✳ **Outcome** Buzzing taste buds, Thai cooking tips and an extremely tight waistband ✳ **Where** Chiang Mai, northern Thailand

WHAT TO EXPECT

Step out of your shoes and into a Thai home, where the dining table is set for eight, even though it's only 11am. You've followed instructions and skipped breakfast, so your belly rumbles as you join your fellow classmates in the kitchen at a row of wok-burners and a central bench – your workspace for the next four hours.

Your Thai cooking class started a couple of hours ago at Chiang Mai's lively market, where your teacher took you on a tour of the stalls, pointing out handy kitchen implements and favourite premade pastes, perfect foodie souvenirs all going for a song. This doubled as a lesson in ingredient identification – bulbous turmeric, galangal and a dizzying array of tofu varieties.

Back in the kitchen, a cracking pace is set as you work your way through seven dishes – from appetiser to curry paste to dessert. You learn the value of a cleaver, the functions of differently shaped mortar and pestles, what gives papaya salad its tantalising zing and how many chillies are the right number for heat without tears.

The first surprise is how easy it is to get the right balance of spicy, salty, sour and sweet – the four tastes integral to Thai cuisine. The second is how much fun it is to cook with a group of strangers. The third: how much you can eat in one day without bursting (six meals, anyone?).

As each dish is cooked, you sit down together and eat. It's a progressive meal punctuated by bursts of frenzied kitchen activity. At the end of the day you'll be stuffed and proud – and inspired to raid your local Asian supermarket for tamarind paste, palm sugar and *phrik ki noo* (bird shit chilli).

How it suits you

The organised traveller will love the precision – ingredients are perfectly portioned and your teacher will keep firm control of proceedings, calling instructions and keeping time like a culinary sergeant major. Social travellers will enjoy the dinner-party feel – there's plenty of time to get to know each other, exchange stories and gather great travel tips (especially food-based ones) with your fellow amateur chefs. The take-home cookbook will appeal to all.

What you'll get from it

★ **Cooking confidence** Once you've created a delicious pad thai, stir-fried prawns with tamarind or sticky rice pudding for yourself in 15 minutes flat, a whole world of Thai cooking opens up.

★ **Local insight** You'll get a feel for the context of Thai cuisine as the locals enjoy it: based around a daily visit to the market to buy what's fresh, built around a perfect balance of flavours, cooked quickly to retain the intensity and texture of the ingredients.

★ **Killer biceps** The correct length of pounding to create curry paste of the right consistency is 20 minutes.

Practical details

There are plenty of operators in Chiang Mai; **Basil Cookery School** (basilcookery.com) and **Thai Farm Cooking School** (thaifarmcooking.net) are both recommended, with courses held year-round.

Other options

There are cooking schools of every flavour in Bangkok, and you'll find classes in other Thai tourist centres like Phuket and Koh Samui too. Try **Thai Cooking School** (thaicookingschool.co.uk) in London or **Temple of Thai** (www.templeofthai.com) in the US, or look up local Thai cooking classes in your home town.

Doing it at home

Visit your local Asian market and stock up on supplies (they all should be listed in your take-home cookbook), then aim to cook a new recipe each week – plenty of them are quick and easy, perfect for after-work meals. When you've perfected a few recipes, throw a Thai-themed dinner party.

See how seriously Thais take their food at Chiang Mai's night market, the perfect place to pick up the taste-bud-tingling secrets of creating Thai food at home.

Grab a bite to eat as you shop for fresh produce.

LEARN THE LINGO
IN GUATEMALA

Duration Two to six weeks ✷ **Cost** US$200 to US$300 per week ✷ **Outcome** A second language, Latin soul and a weapon against Alzheimer's ✷ **Where** Antigua, Guatemala

After a few lessons, have a yarn with Mayans at the local textile market.

For wanderers who want to talk the talk as well as walk the walk, Antigua is the place to learn Spanish, the sweetest of tongues.

WHAT TO EXPECT

Imagine being able to speak to people in their native language, whether they're from San Francisco, Tierra del Fuego, Africa's west coast or the foothills of San Sebastián. Now, imagine going from your repertoire of *'buenos días'* and *'hasta la vista,* baby' to fluent, if not perfect, conversational Spanish in a few short weeks.

Spanish is one of the world's fastest-growing languages, with 500 million speakers in at least 22 countries – including at least 50 million in the US. The best place to join the party is Antigua – the cheapest, friendliest and certainly one of the prettiest cities in which to learn Spanish, where cobbled streets and perfectly preserved colonial architecture are spread at the foot of a majestic volcano.

This Unesco World Heritage–listed city is filled with language schools that offer five hours of one-on-one language instruction per day. Students are housed in local homes, where they become part of family life, practising to say *'Me podrías pasar la sal, por favor?'* ('Could you please pass the salt?') with their new brothers and sisters.

On weekends, Antigua is the perfect place to enjoy a gentle stroll, a *café con leche* in the quiet main square or even a hike up the active Volcano Pacaya nearby.

How it suits you

Learning a second language expands your mind, lets you into the subconscious of another culture, and even wards off Alzheimer's! Living with a Guatemalan family and having your own personal teacher means you'll be prattling on before you know it, making this experience ideal for chatty, outgoing types who want to be able to use their formidable social skills on the Spanish-speaking peoples of the earth. But it can also work for the nerdy closet linguist, for whom tracing the complex patterns of a new grammar will be a source of endless satisfaction.

What you'll get from it

★ **Discipline** You'll get out of this what you put into it: the more you study and practise, the better you'll speak.
★ **Brain gain** Brain plasticity means that learning a new language has hidden cognitive benefits, like delaying the onset of dementia and enhancing multitasking skills.
★ **Immersion** You'll learn in a few weeks what would take you years with language tapes or group lessons at home, and your friendly Guatemalan family will embrace you like one of their own.
★ **A chance to explore** Antigua is a perfect base for trips to Guatemala's Pacific and Atlantic coasts, Tikal's Mayan ruins, Lake Atitlán and Chichicastenango's handicraft markets.

Practical details

Most of Antigua's schools have websites, and each offers a different package that includes teaching, meals and lodging with a local family. Some, like **Academia de Español Probigua** (probigua.org), donate their profits to local rural communities, while others, like **Proyecto Lingüístico Francisco Marroquín** (spanishschoolplfm.com), run projects to preserve Guatemala's indigenous languages.

Other options

There are Spanish schools in other Guatemalan towns and cities, and in most large cities throughout the Spanish-speaking world. To learn Spanish outside Spain and Latin America, look up your local **Instituto Cervantes** (www.cervantes.es).

Doing it at home

Spanish-speakers are everywhere, so you'll have no trouble finding an ear for your massive new vocabulary. Head to your local tapas bar or *taquería,* or just go see the latest Almodóvar movie – your friends will be impressed when you tell them you don't need to bother with subtitles.

DISCOVER THE RHYTHM OF THE RUMBA IN CUBA

Duration Five days ✳ **Cost** From £70 ✳ **Outcome** Lithe limbs, polished footwork and the satisfaction of earning your Cuba kudos on rumba's native turf ✳ **Where** Santiago de Cuba & Havana

Perfect the art of flirty footwork set to percussion-driven rhythm-and-groove in the spiritual home of rumba.

WHAT TO EXPECT

Get ready to limber up and summon the persona of a lusty dockworker – there's nothing more raw, earthy and sexually charged than a Cuban rumba in full and frenzied flow.

Rumba is a courtship dance rooted in the warehouses of the port of Matanzas, east of Havana, where dockworkers from African brotherhoods would bang cod boxes, thwack spoons and tap shipbuilders' pegs – anything to create a rhythm. As the crowd thickened around the *rumbero* couple, the dance would intensify, the chanting reach a crescendo and the percussion-driven music ramp up.

To learn the rumba, you'll need to leave your inhibitions at home and be hot to trot and on the ball – no room for a mojito hangover here! Guys should wear comfortable clothes, leaving them free to writhe to the full repertoire of moves and mime the action of cutting sugarcane with a machete. Girls should dress in a flouncy skirt full enough to swirl and flick.

The *guaguancó*, the most popular of the three dances of rumba, pivots around a virile man's pursuit of a woman who does her best to resist and repel the male overture with a coquettish dancing stance. As he gestures – normally with a pelvic thrust called a *vacunao* – she covers herself with a modest hand in quick response.

Once you've mastered the moves, join any spontaneous rumba session that erupts across courtyards and streets on the island of Cuba.

How it suits you

Cubans are some of the most confident people on the planet, and this experience will most appeal to the passionate, outgoing and adventurous traveller. There's no place for bashfulness, restrained moves and tone-deaf ears in a rumba session. If you travel for music, the wild and untamed energy of a rumba session will leave you panting for more fast-paced performance.

What you'll get from it

★ **Dating wisdom** There'll be no more beating about the romantic bush, because the *guaguancó* rumba will furnish you with all the right flirting techniques.

★ **Precision** Whenever a rumba kicks off, you'll pump that fancy footwork like a true virtuoso. Your name and the words 'uncoordinated' and 'limbs' will never again be uttered in the same sentence.

★ **Musical mastery** In Cuba, music is king. Now that you know your rumba from your reggaeton, you'll be able to impress your amigos with your musical repertoire.

Practical details

Càlédöñiâ (www.caledonialanguages.co.uk) organises individual rumba lessons in Santiago de Cuba with the highly talented Ballet Folklórico Cutumba, and group lessons in Havana with tutors from the performing arts college.

Other options

Salsa Caribe (salsacaribe.co.uk) runs regular Sunday rumba classes in north London, while **AlbaCubaDance** (albacubadance.co.uk) has classes for group and private rumba and Afro-Cuban lessons in Edinburgh and elsewhere in the UK. For rumba classes in Seattle, try the **Academy of Cuban Folklore & Dance** (cubanfolkloricdance.com).

Doing it at home

Now that you've honed the art of shoulder rippling and choreographed pelvic thrusts, throw open your patio doors to the neighbours and let your drum-playing friends ignite the flame of the emotive rumba game.

Fancy footwork: dancing the rumba in Havana's Callejon de Hamel.

SHAKE UP A PERFECT
COCKTAIL IN NEW YORK

Duration One week ✳ **Cost** US$3500 ✳ **Outcome** Cocktail know-how and a packed social life
– now that you can make all the classics, you're on everyone's invite list ✳ **Where** New York City, US

Shaken or stirred, sir?
Pouring a martini at New York's
Algonquin Hotel.

The Rainbow Room, Park Plaza, *Mad Men* ... need we say more? In New York, a city long identified as the epicentre of cocktail culture, you need not only visit Manhattan, you can also learn how to make one.

WHAT TO EXPECT

Pop quiz: what's the difference between Plymouth and London-style gin? How do you make a Sidecar? And what cocktail was invented during Prohibition?

Deconstructing mixed drinks is art, science and history rolled into one. But cramming your head with an encyclopaedic amount of knowledge in mixology class is infinitely more satisfying than school, and a whole lot more fun.

The course starts with seminars that provide you with in-depth knowledge across the vast range of spirits – the nitty gritty on their origins, production and properties, grounded in cultural history – and you begin to understand that all gins, vodkas and whiskies are not created equal. The result is a solid foundation in the spirits that are the building blocks of the beloved cocktail, taught by some of the spirit world's most lauded experts.

While this is deliciously fascinating stuff (your palate is performing admirably through all the blind tastings), you're not just there to drink it all in. You're getting hands-on with the tools and techniques of mixology: muddling, pouring, layering, blending, shaking and stirring your way to an impressive repertoire of refreshments.

You're also learning how to pair drinks with food and how to critique cocktail menus. And like any good mixologist, you can now wax eloquent about the evolution of everyone's favourite drinks. And the pièce de résistance? You're putting it all together to create your own libations.

How it suits you

If you're a discerning consumer, once you're equipped with the tools and knowledge to DIY, you'll no longer have to go cross-country for your favourite drink. If you're a social butterfly aiming to become a professional mixologist, you're in your element: inspired by the energy and extraversion in the room, you're ready to start your own drink-of-the-month club.

What you'll get from it

★ **Precision** The devil is in the details and the best way to impress the palate is with precision. And now, having graduated to a higher standard, you can now scorn the amateurs who pulverise the mint in their mojitos.

★ **Imagination** Having deconstructed the classic American cocktails that have endured the test of time (even Prohibition), you're bubbling over with ideas for the next big drink.

★ **Social skills** It's become second-nature for you to engineer multiple bespoke cocktails while straightening your tie and discussing politics, business and art: yep, you're ready for a role on *Mad Men*.

Practical details

Manhattan's **Beverage Alcohol Resource** (beveragealcoholresource.com) runs a unique, in-depth program once yearly, offering two levels of certification, chosen by participants after the course begins. Note that the legal drinking age in the US is 21.

Other options

Try the molecular mixology course at **Shaker Bar Schools** (shaker-uk.com) in London, Birmingham, Belfast, Cape Town and Johannesburg. Australia's **Bar Max** (barmax.com.au) offers a four-hour cocktail course in Sydney and the surrounding area.

Doing it at home

Grab some vintage glasses, print up menus and invite people over for an old-fashioned cocktail party, featuring classics as well as your own concoctions. Eschew the beer and wine and revive the hospitality of yesteryear by setting up a wet bar to 'fix drinks' when friends drop in unexpectedly.

TUNE UP FOR A GAMELAN GROOVE IN JAVA

Duration A month of weekly lessons ✱ **Cost** US$70 ✱ **Outcome** A broadened musical horizon and a sense of instruments as living things ✱ **Where** Yogyakarta, Indonesia

Join a gamelan orchestra in Yogyakarta and become a part of the music described as 'the stirring of a thousand bells'.

WHAT TO EXPECT

Watching a gamelan performance in Java is one thing, but taking part in one will really immerse you in a musical style described by a poet as akin to 'moonlight or flowing water'.

A beginner's course at Yogyakarta State University will introduce you to the many and varied gamelan instruments, give you some basic skills and train you in reading Javanese gamelan notation (gamelan operates on a completely different pitch to Western music). The course concludes with a public performance.

The city of Yogyakarta (pronounced 'Jogjakarta') is where the Javanese language is purest, Java's arts brightest and its traditions most visible. One of the most delightful of these artistic traditions is gamelan, so where better to learn the ropes than the city that's central to Java's creative and intellectual heritage?

A gamelan orchestra is mainly made up of metallic percussion instruments, with a few woodwinds or strings thrown in. Each gamelan set is considered an entity, and is tuned to its own particular pitch: you would never play the instruments on their own or mix them up with another set.

A gamelan set is thought to possess mystical power, hence its use in ritual, including weddings and rain-making ceremonies. It also appears in theatres and palaces, and in traditional shadow puppetry.

How it suits you

Artistic types will enjoy adding their mite to the gorgeous, susurrating sound produced by a gamelan orchestra. Spiritual types will enter into the meditative experience of playing this hypnotic, fluid music, while social butterflies will relish the strong group focus of the orchestra. Conversely, this might be one for loners: a chance to be around people without having to talk to them!

What you'll get from it

★ **Instant gratification** Gamelan, as opposed to many musical styles, is relatively easy to pick up. All you need to participate is a good sense of rhythm.

★ **A group high** Playing in a gamelan orchestra is particularly conducive to the group dynamic. There is no conductor; the musicians follow the lead of the drummer. Listening to one another and the collective sound is what it's all about, and each player is equally valued.

★ **Reverence** Gamelan is all about ritual: note that players always walk around their instruments, rather than stepping over them, and they bow to senior players. It all lends a beautifully mystical air to the experience.

Practical details

The gamelan courses at **Yogyakarta State University** (io. uny.ac.id/course) usually run between June and August, but it's possible to request tuition outside of those months. There needs to be eight participants for the course to go ahead.

Other options

Now you've got the taste for a different sound, take your exotic music studies further with bagpipe lessons in Scotland with **Scotia Pipers** (scotiapipers.co.uk) or a **tabla** course in India – the town of Rishikesh is well supplied with teachers; just ask at your hotel or guesthouse for a recommendation.

Doing it at home

The West's love affair with gamelan has been going on for some time now, so you might find an orchestra that's looking for new players. Or try asking at your local universities, which sometimes buy gamelan sets. Failing that, try buying yourself some recordings, or even a wind chime – it will give you that same beautiful effect.

Pick an instrument and become part of a gamelan ensemble.

ROCK AND ROLL AT ROLLER DERBY SCHOOL

Duration Five days ✳ **Cost** Free (donations welcome) ✳ **Outcome** Build rock-hard glutes and let out some steam while perfecting your crossovers ✳ **Where** Pomona and Pleasanton, California, US

Expect a few bumps and bruises by the end of your roller derby day.

Don't let rules and elbows get in the way of a good time as you roll over the competition on eight tiny wheels.

Roller derby is a game of skill ... and controlled violence. Anyone can pummel someone to the ground, but try doing it while careening around a track on roller skates.

Roller derby hit it big in Chicago in 1935 with its heart-stopping blend of speed and theatrics, performed on a circular ramp 3.5 metres across and tilted an unsettling 42 degrees. It was the first sport where women got paid to compete, and for the most part it's remained dominated by female skaters, though today there are thousands of co-ed and even all-male teams all over the world.

From the San Francisco Bay Bombers to the Los Angeles Firebirds, the biggest names in professional banked track roller-derby skate in California. Their league, the American Roller Skating Derby, puts on boot camps at the teams' home tracks every couple of months. Visitors can also join in open practices.

To join in, you have to be between 16 and 45, own a good pair of quad roller skates (inline wheels are OK for your first time) and carry valid medical insurance. Don't worry if you're not in the best shape. The practice runs kick you into gear, and a little extra body weight comes in handy for slamming opponents into the rail.

First you'll get to grips with footwork, and learn how to get up safely when you've been knocked down – which you will be, again and again. Once you're steady enough not to become road kill, you'll move on to jumping, sliding, blocking (when you slam into an opponent) and whipping (when you slingshot a teammate with an arm or leg). Just remember: tripping is illegal. If the ref sees it ...

How it suits you

Roller derby is a game for speed demons, former skateboarders and skaters, and anyone with guts. Bring your taste for adventure and reckless abandon. A game that is also known as 'wrestling on wheels', it also presents a great opportunity to unbridle your inner Hulk. But if you have a low threshold for pain, bring a well-padded pair of shorts, along with a dependable helmet and sturdy knee pads and wrist guards. Padding will be your new best friend, along with your new teammates, Skinny Minny Miller and Ice Box.

What you'll get from it

★ **Speed** Remember how it felt to skate as fast as you could down the driveway? Now imagine that caress of the wind on your cheeks as the opposing team eats your dust.

★ **Strength** Pushing those heavy skates around for three hours is a great cardiovascular and core workout.

★ **Satisfaction** Where else are you rewarded for hip checking people out of the way?

★ **Freedom** Permission to be the terror on wheels you were born to be.

Practical details

American Roller Skating Derby (arsdbombers.com) training camps are held throughout the year in California, on both indoor (Pomona FairPlex, Building 9) and outdoor (Alameda County Fairgrounds, Pleasanton) banked tracks. Joining in is free, though donations that will go towards maintaining the tracks are very welcome.

Other options

Look for impromptu training sessions in Las Vegas, Chicago, New York and Orlando, Florida, or catch one of the league's games held throughout the year. There are also roller-derby training camps in Chilliwack (Canada), New Plymouth (New Zealand) and Brisbane (Australia).

Doing it at home

Find the local league's website and check for boot camps, open practices and games, then consider trying out for the team. Even if you decide to hang up the skates, you'll always have your body-slamming derby persona to channel if you need it.

WALK WITH WOLVES IN SLOVAKIA'S MOUNTAINS

Duration One to three weeks ✳ **Cost** From €750 ✳ **Outcome** Lessons on conserving Europe's mountain wildlife, après-ski fun in an idyllic lodge ✳ **Where** Nízky Tatry National Park, Slovakia

WHAT TO EXPECT

Join a scheme that brings together locals, volunteers, hunters, conservationists and conflicting interests in the remote landscape of the Carpathian Mountains, all in the cause of accurately monitoring mountain species: grey wolves, lynx, wildcat, brown bear and the iconic European goat-antelope, the chamois.

The Carpathian Mountains are best known for skiing, but the region harbours the highest concentration of Europe's wildest beasts and most-endangered wildlife. This makes it Europe's top spot for tracking and working with wildlife, particularly predators.

You'll be out in the sticks in Central Europe's most stunning scenery, keeping tabs on these high-altitude animals. You'll work in terrain as remote as Europe gets, in dense forests and high mountains, often under thick snow. Instructors advise on everything from snow-scaling to bear-spotting, and you can follow your winter wildlife crash course with a summertime chamois-focused project.

Estimates of wolf and lynx populations vary, and your main mission is helping ascertain accurate numbers. DNA samples you'll collect will lead to the scheme's better understanding of the animals' movements and diet.

In the evening, break up the hard graft at your accommodation: an alpine lodge with sublime views, and catering included. And because isolation affects the most enthusiastic eco-volunteers, chamois-monitoring comes with a 36-hour break in which you can hike to Jasna, Slovakia's key ski area. Beasts *and* pistes. Purr-fection!

How it suits you

Party animals, creature-comfort cravers: retreat now. This is strictly for adventure-lovers, isolation junkies and, as you'll be covering 10km to 20km daily in rugged terrain, the pretty damned fit. Winter sports enthusiasts should listen up too: snow-negotiating is an important part of the process and Jasna's ski slopes are temptingly close.

What you'll get from it

★ **Tracker instinct** Your ability to spot beasts and birds will morph from clues like footprints to the ultimate prize: full-on visuals.

★ **Alpine break** There's still time for time off: when that arrives, you're in some of Europe's most pristine mountain scenery.

★ **Awareness** If you thought wildlife conservation was a walk in the park, you'll rethink and gain a sense of the mountain conservationists invariably have to climb in order to achieve their goals.

★ **Once-in-a-lifetime experience** Volunteer experiences are for limited periods in January and June, and are on offer only until the completion of five-year monitoring cycles in 2015.

Practical details

The **Slovak Wildlife Society** (slovakwildlife.org) master-mind excursions with British conservation trust **BTCV** (tcv.org.uk). Pick-up/drop off to Bratislava train station is included.

Other options

Conservation Volunteers (conservationvolunteers.com.au) in Australia runs Wild Futures, an initiative striving to protect a dozen endangered Australian species, which regularly requires volunteers. **Bunac** (bunac.org), in the UK and US, organises many conservation projects for volunteers worldwide, including looking after lions in South Africa.

Doing it at home

Before embarking for pastures new to help preserve the planet's wildlife, try it in your garden. Grassroots stuff like choosing native plants or leaving logs, tree stumps or an untrimmed patch on your lawn gives your own turf the natural look, and gives local fauna and flora a chance to thrive.

De Agostini / Getty Images ©

Join the annual project that monitors Europe's wildest beasts – wolves, lynxes, bears and chamois – and learn how to collect DNA samples as an animal tracker extraordinaire.

No need to be afraid: Europe's wolves need all the support they can get.

ADD A STRING TO YOUR BOW IN MONGOLIA

Duration Nine days ✸ **Cost** £1995 ✸ **Outcome** Improved eye–hand coordination, archery skills and the stature of Genghis Khan ✸ **Where** Outside Ulaanbaatar, Mongolia

Make like an ancient warrior with target practice Mongolian-style, and enjoy the far horizons in the Land of Blue Sky.

WHAT TO EXPECT

Archery is big in Mongolia, as you'd expect from a culture that was once largely nomadic, often at war and all about the horse. Why not get a taste of what it's like to be a proud, bow-wielding warrior (even if you're not 'manly' – there are plenty of gifted women archers in Mongolia) with some Genghis Khan warrior training?

Archery figures large in Mongolian folk legends, like the one about the great archer who shot down six suns to save his people from drought. It also forms a crucial part of the country's famous Naadam Festival; along with wrestling and horse-racing, it's one of the 'three manly sports' featured there.

There's plenty of romance attached to this sport, too. Following tradition, archers use a bent bow made of layered horn, bark and wood; the arrows are made of willow and the feathers from birds of prey; the targets are leather. The scorers have a special form of singing that lets the archers know from a distance how they're doing.

Try Mongolian archery out in a low-key way by taking a homestay trip, heading out for a spot of target practice with your hosts, or don the traditional 'deel' costume à la Genghis Khan and combine the sport with a shamanic ceremony, horse-lassoing and battle strategy.

How it suits you

Adventurous types will relish getting out into the endless plains and practising this ancient sport where it all began. Spiritual types may want to infuse their archery with a little meditation, like the Zen archers of Japan. Perhaps you're a historical type? You can make believe you're an archer in the Mongol armies that once swept the world before them.

What you'll get from it

★ **An eagle eye** All that focusing on targets trains your eye to greater precision.
★ **A noble bearing** You just can't help but puff out your chest a little when you're taking aim with a bow in the land where the bow is king.
★ **A sense of distance** One of rural Mongolia's great beauties is its sense of expansive space. The rush of your arrow in flight is a very concrete way to connect with those horizons.

Practical details

High and Wild (www.highandwild.co.uk) runs Genghis Khan Warrior Training sessions between late June and September. Homestay trips are offered by **Ger to Ger** (gertoger.org).

Other options

Now you've tried archery in Mongolia, why not try it in Tibet, or Japan, or … France? Archery-focused travel is well-catered for: just try Googling 'archery holidays'.

Doing it at home

It may lack the romance of your Mongolian experience, but you can still practise archery when you return to your own brand of civilisation. Join a club and keep honing those target skills.

The Mongolian archery
champion shows how it's done;
national costume is optional.

KEEP A POKER FACE AT
VEGAS CARD SCHOOL

Duration Four weeks ❋ **Cost** US$300 ❋ **Outcome** Card-dealing skills, sleight of hand and Casino Royale style ❋ **Where** Las Vegas, Nevada, US

How it suits you

Adrenalin junkies will soon be addicted to the intensity of high-stakes games, while those who like to be in charge will appreciate commanding a table. Maths nerds will delight in counting cards and keeping track of multiple players.

What you'll get from it

★ **A winning streak** You'll know blackjack so well you'll be a top player, and bring in some extra money playing at a local casino.

★ **Job skills** You'll be qualified to deal blackjack at a casino, a skill that travels to wherever there are casinos.

★ **Party tricks** Impress your friends with your rapid dealing and counting.

Practical details

PCI Dealer School (pcidealerschool.com) in Vegas offers classes for dealing blackjack and other card games. Enrolment is open and start times are rolling.

Other options

In Australia and New Zealand, the **SKYCITY** (skycity. snaphire.com) resort trains blackjack dealers to work at their casinos. The training is free. In the US, head to other known gambling towns such as Reno or Atlantic City for hands-on career training. The **Casino Gaming Institute** (casinogaminginst.com) has campuses across the East Coast.

Doing it at home

Show off your new dealing skills by hosting a casino party where you'll deal for the house, of course. Blackjack night once a week with friends is another way to keep your skills refreshed, or you could simply change careers by applying for a blackjack-dealing job.

WHAT TO EXPECT

The dusty Nevada desert is interrupted by the glitter of party town Las Vegas, where 24-hour casinos bling and clang along the Vegas Strip. Slot machines dispense coins with a clatter, while crowds gather around high-stakes games of craps or roulette. But the silent intensity of blackjack is archetypical Vegas. Entire movies like *21* and scenes

Play your hand on the other side of the table, skilfully shuffling and dealing with the cool lightning-fast style that defines Las Vegas dealers.

in films including *The Hangover* and *Rainman* depict the game's vulnerability to card counting, where the big money can be made.

Learn blackjack's tricks and strategies at Nevada's oldest casino dealing school, and earn the respect of players as a dealer at the head of the table. At a professional training school you'll learn all the skills required: not only the rules of the game, but also how to quickly shuffle and total cards, how to split chips and how to work with multiple decks. Classes are also held in the art of dealing baccarat, poker and roulette, and in the roll of the dice.

Classes are held in a casino-like setting to give a feel of the real-life pressures of the job. Once it's completed you'll be qualified to start as an entry-level dealer, working smaller casinos until you've dealt enough cards to move up to the big houses on the Strip.

Where better to sharpen your card skills than the world's gambling mecca?

EARN A JUMBO EDUCATION IN THAILAND

Duration Two to 10 days ✳ **Cost** 5800 to 35,000 baht ✳ **Outcome** Gain an exotic skill and become conversant in elephant ✳ **Where** Lampang, northern Thailand

You'll never forget bonding with these amazing beasts; nor will your elephant!

Climb aboard your own private elephant in northern Thailand, and learn what it takes to care for, command and fall in love with these priceless pachyderms.

WHAT TO EXPECT

It's full immersion, elephant-style, from the time you begin at the Thai Elephant Conservation Center in Lampang. After memorising the 14 Thai commands that will have you fluent in pachyderm, you'll be apprenticed to a *mahout* and elephant. For the length of your stay, this human and mountain will be your working companions.

You're now responsible for your elephant's wellbeing – getting it fed, washing it, riding it out into the forest each night where it sleeps, preparing it for the centre's daily tourist shows – until you depart, by which time you'll quite possibly be in love with this big bag of grey skin.

Your first duty will be to wash your elephant, riding it down into a soupy brown lake swimming with elephant turds that bear an unfortunate resemblance to croutons. Balancing on your elephant's back as it rolls and rocks is work itself – and watch out for anyone around you who knows the command *baan baan,* or you'll soon be sprayed with a trunkful of water.

After three days of training, it's show time. Literally. At the daily tourist show, you'll be in command of your big-footed friend, issuing the commands and helping it perform its signature trick before taking a bow at curtain call – the elephant gets all the congratulatory sugar cane, sorry.

How it suits you

For the leader of the gang, what greater power trip than to be in control of one of the world's largest land mammals? Three tonnes of lumbering flesh is yours to command. No Hummer could ever compete. And if you're an animal lover, prepare the heartstrings because the centre's main *raison d'être* is as Thailand's first and foremost elephant hospital. Most of the animals you'll encounter were rescued and treated after injury, often making them incapable of surviving back in the wild.

What you'll get from it

★ **Unity** By about the third day you'll start to feel as though you and the elephant are one.
★ **Precision** Get the intonation wrong, or lose the respect of your elephant, and it'll be a pair of puzzled eyes that stare back at you from behind the trunk.
★ **Interaction** Days spent not just with an elephant but with your own mahout give you a window into local life.
★ **Language** At any point, at any place, you'll be able to command anyone in Thai to lie on their stomach or spray water.

Practical details

The **Thai Elephant Conservation Center,** Lampang, runs courses year-round, offered for two, three or 10 days. Further information is available on **Changthai.com** (changthai.com), a website operated by a centre employee.

Other options

In Canada, work as a sea-lion trainer for a day at **Marine Life** (wem.ca) in West Edmonton Mall. Become an intern at the **PAWS** (paws.org) wildlife rehabilitation centre in the US, or try volunteering as a wildlife researcher at a game reserve in South Africa.

Doing it at home

It's unlikely you'll have an elephant on hand in your backyard, so keep practising the commands and plan for a second trip to the Conservation Center. Serial *mahouts* are not uncommon here.

MEDITATE WITH MONKS
IN SOUTH KOREA

Duration One day ✳ **Cost** From W20,000 ✳ **Outcome** A 24-hour health cleanse, self-reflection and strategies for coping with life's daily stresses ✳ **Where** South Korea

WHAT TO EXPECT

If you've ever wanted to drape yourself in robes, go vego and give a Buddhist lifestyle a go, with no strings attached, the Jogye Order of Korean Buddhism gives you the chance to experience the daily life of a Buddhist monk in temples across South Korea. Most of these complexes are historic and dazzling pieces of architecture, often located in leafy national or provincial parks.

Attired in a set of loose cotton clothing, you'll follow the monks' daily rituals, including periods of Seon (Zen) meditation and taking part in the three daily services, one of which begins before dawn and involves a body-challenging 108 prostrations.

Here's your chance to learn some temple etiquette, such as how to greet your fellow monks with a bow and hands clasped in prayer to your chest. Instructions are in Korean – locals like to take time out from their routines by spending a night at a temple – but at many temples there is someone on hand to translate into English. Don't panic if you don't get everything; you can easily pick up the main elements of temple etiquette by just looking and learning.

While enjoying three hearty, shared vegetarian meals, you'll be taught how not to waste one grain of rice. Daily activities to promote self-reflection include sweeping the temple grounds in the early morning, making paper lanterns in the shape of lotus flowers and enjoying the elements of a traditional tea ceremony. You'll soon be starting on that path towards inner peace.

How it suits you

If you're spiritually and culturally inquisitive, the Templestay program is ideal. Your comfort zones may be challenged: sleeping quarters and bathrooms will be shared, food is all vegetarian and there are long periods where you'll be expected to kneel. The emphasis is on self-reflection so this is also an ideal activity for those seeking quiet time.

What you'll get from it

★ **Healthier body** This is a chance to give your body time off from daily strains and stresses. The Buddhist way eschews meat, alcohol and drugs, including smoking.

★ **Supple limbs** Chairs are not an option. Expect your legs and back to ache (in a good way!) after sitting crossed-legged on the floor or kneeling for long periods.

Practical details

At least two weeks before you plan to join a **Templestay** (templestay.com) program, log onto the organisation's website to find a temple location that suits. Not all temples offer the same program and some are easier to reach by public transport than others. Typically, the programs run for 24 hours, but longer or shorter stays can be arranged for those who have more or less time.

Other options

Venture to sacred **Mt Koya** (www.koya.org), where you can stay in temple lodgings with Japanese monks. Closer to home, go on retreat into the English countryside at **Madhyamaka** (madhyamaka.org) or check into the **Shambhala Meditation Centre** (pioneervalley.shambhala.org) in Pioneer Valley, Massachusetts.

Doing it at home

If your day as a monk has inspired you to delve deeper, create your own temple at home and take up a vegetarian diet. The ideal of clearing the mind of all thoughts during meditation takes years of practice, so don't worry if it seems elusive at first. Practise at home, and you'll master the breathing exercises and sitting positions reasonably quickly.

Spend 24 hours with South Korea's Buddhist monks, and experience a centuries-old way of life in one of the country's most beautiful temples.

Feeling the force – young monks at Jogyesa Temple in Seoul.

BEND IRON TO YOUR
WILL IN WALES

Duration One or two days ✳ **Cost** £130 to £260 ✳ **Outcome** Use brute strength to mould metal and learn a new party trick to astound your friends ✳ **Where** Carmarthenshire, Wales

Turn back time at the blacksmith's hearth.

Harness the power of fire just as our ancestors did, and handcraft your own ironwork using ancient blacksmithing artistry in the Celtic heartland of Wales.

Step away from the Ikea flat pack. If you really want to prove your metal, go into battle with metal itself and wield your hammer like a pro. You'll wind up knowing your anvil from your forge, and get to hit stuff really hard.

You don't have to be a pumped-up body-builder to bend metal. This two-day blacksmithing beginner course will have you hand-forging your own ironwork with confidence and skill, if not artistry, as you step back in time to the age before mass production.

Once there was a smithy in every British village, and the steady bang and hiss of metal echoed across the land. In fact, blacksmithing was such a common profession that it endowed the English-speaking world with the profusion of people still known as 'Smith' today. Whether or not Smith is your surname, learning this noble trade allows you to reconnect with your make-it-yourself roots.

You'll learn to use the forge (the blacksmith's hearth) to heat your metal and see iron transform to hissing sparkler-white. With hammer in hand, you'll form angles and curves to change your piece of metal into a thing of beauty (or at least something recognisable). Yes, you have conquered the elements. Take a bow.

How it suits you

Look, honey! I made it myself. Do-it-yourself fanatics, you're about to enter the pearly gates of DIY heaven. When you arrive back home brandishing the brackets made by your very own hands, fix-it guru-dom will be complete. And for us emotional types? Sometimes we don't need to continually talk round in circles. Sometimes we just need to bang things. Bang them for an extended period. Bang them really hard ...

What you'll get from it

★ **Boasting rights** Yeah, I just love your new candlesticks. Where did you get them from? Oh really, that's nice. I made mine myself.

★ **Discover ancient skills** The craft of hand-forging ironwork has a history that stretches back to the early Celts, so it seems appropriate to learn the artistry of blacksmithing in the Celtic heartland.

★ **Blow off steam** It's cheaper than a therapist. Strike hammer to anvil and feel your tension dissipate.

Practical details

Aaron Petersen (ferricfusion.co.uk) runs regular one- and two-day blacksmithing courses in St Clears, near Carmarthen in Carmarthenshire. Participants need to provide their own steel-capped boots.

Other options

In Canada, the **Wareham Forge** (warehamforge.ca) in central Ontario offers weekend courses in introductory blacksmithing, as well as more advanced metalwork training. In Australia, learn basic blacksmithing at Ray Gard's **Raven Forge** (raven-forge.com.au) in Victoria. **Mojo Metal Design** (mojometaldesign.com), near Clonakilty in County Cork, provides training for the novice blacksmith in Ireland.

Doing it at home

Say goodbye to the mass-produced and embark on an exploration into what you can do by yourself. Harness your new zeal for the homemade and conquer all those little household projects you once put aside.

HEAL WITH YOUR HANDS
IN BANGKOK

Duration From five days ✳ **Cost** 9500 baht ✳ **Outcome** Ancient knowledge, inner understanding and fingers that melt away stress like butter ✳ **Where** Wat Po, Bangkok, Thailand

How it suits you

Learning ancient arts from Buddhist masters will certainly appeal to travellers of a spiritual disposition, but you don't have be captivated by Eastern philosophy to benefit. Plenty of people come to Wat Po to learn a practical skill to apply at home – with the stresses of modern living, who wouldn't appreciate having Thai massage on tap in the living room?

What you'll get from it

★ **Technique** Learning your way around the human body takes time and training – that's what makes the difference between magic fingers and kneading dough for bread rolls.
★ **Understanding** The 'why' is as important as the 'how' in Thai massage; rubbing sore muscles without knowing the cause of the pain would be like treating a broken leg with an aspirin.
★ **Knowledge** Thousands of years of wisdom have been distilled to create *nuat phaen boran*; you can't learn it all in a week, but studying with trained masters will set you on the right path.

Practical details

Wat Po Thai Traditional Medical School (watpomassage. com) is tucked away at the back of the Wat Po monastery, seconds from the Tha Tien ferry pier on the Chao Phraya river. Multiday courses start daily, year-round.

Other options

You don't have to stop at massage – Wat Po also runs courses in aromatherapy and traditional Thai herbal medicine. In India, sip from a different fount of knowledge on an ayurvedic massage course in Kerala. Or head to Tokyo to learn the fundamentals of Shiatsu massage with lessons at **Japan Shiatsu College** (e.shiatsu.ac.jp).

Doing it at home

Five days isn't long enough to give up the day job, but you could start down the road to becoming a professional therapist by training at a local massage centre. Alternatively, come back to Thailand and enrol in the professional course at Wat Po.

WHAT TO EXPECT

You know that feeling of utter relaxation, like sinking into a deep bath at the end of a stressful day? That's what a properly executed massage should feel like. A bad massage, on the other hand, can feel like being mugged with a back-scratcher.

Lots of people *think* they know how to massage – just ask anyone on the dating scene – but learning the real art

There's a healer lurking somewhere inside all of us, and the master masseurs at Bangkok's Wat Po will help you uncover it, with a little Buddhist philosophy thrown in for good measure.

of massage takes time and training. You need to know what not to do, as well as the right buttons to press.

You could always study massage at the local sports centre, but wouldn't it be more satisfying to follow this ancient art back to the source? According to legend, *nuat phaen boran* (traditional Thai massage) was created by Jivaka, the personal physician of the historical Buddha. While a more probable story is that this ancient therapy is a blend of traditions from India and China, the monks of Wat Po have been the official guardians of Thai massage since at least the 18th century.

Recommended as a treatment for everything from stress and fatigue to the symptoms of ageing, Thai massage fuses elements of acupressure, yoga and traditional medicine. The trained masters at Wat Po teach the science and philosophy of massage, as well as the right places to push.

And consider the setting – you'll be walking to class beneath the soaring eaves of Bangkok's best-loved Buddhist monastery.

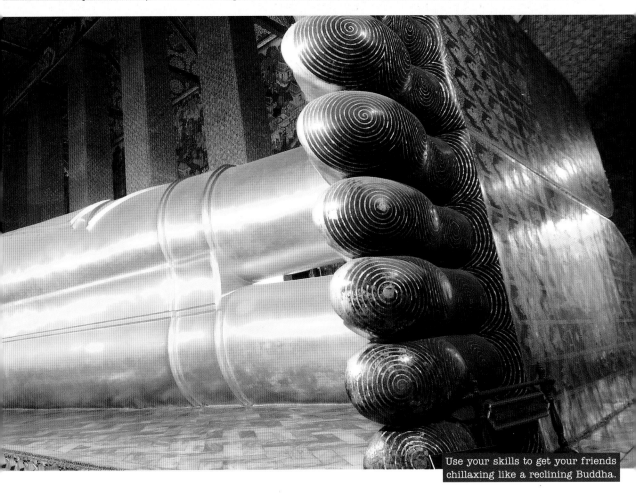

Use your skills to get your friends chillaxing like a reclining Buddha.

MIX SHEEPS-MILK CHEESE IN MALTA

Duration Two days ✳ **Cost** From €136 ✳ **Outcome** Take home tasty handmade cheese and chill out with the sheep and their shepherd ✳ **Where** Xewkija, Gozo, Malta

Get personal with Gozo sheep and their shepherds, embrace their tranquil way of life and learn how to make Malta's traditional sheep's-milk cheese.

WHAT TO EXPECT

On the Maltese island of Gozo – a 20-minute ferry trip from the main island – shepherds can still be found tranquilly patrolling the paths that crisscross the serene countryside or relaxing in the shade as their dogs guard the flocks. Now you can get the lowdown on the sheep-herders' signature cheese and sample the island's pastoral serenity with a private Gozo shepherd experience.

Sheep and their shepherds have been making tracks in Gozo for centuries. Their time-honoured lifestyle might be losing ground to the pressures of modernisation, but shepherds are a conservative lot, preferring traditional practices when it comes to feeding, shearing and hand-milking their ewes.

Your Gozo experience takes place in Xewkija, the oldest village in Gozo, dating back to 1678. Here, on a traditional farm, you'll spend a day working alongside a shepherd and his flock.

With some of the fresh milk you've just helped secure, you'll learn how to prepare Gozo's famous sheep's-milk ġbejniet cheeselets. Your plain cheese (which may later be sun-dried, pickled or rolled in herbs or pepper) won't be ready until the next morning, but you are warmly invited to indulge in a well-earned lunch of other local products accompanying a completed batch of cheeselets and some homemade wine.

How it suits you

Working with animals on a traditional farm, especially first thing in the morning, requires a fair bit of get-up-and-go. You've got to be a do-er, ready to step into the mix of things, even when it involves handling unfamiliar animals or getting your hands dirty doing somewhat icky tasks. Of course, spontaneity is also key: no two days are ever the same when the vagaries of nature come into play.

What you'll get from it

★ **Cultural insight** Joining forces with a shepherd in his home and on his farm provides insights into Gozo's unique cultural heritage.
★ **Food knowledge** You help make the cheese, but at lunch you'll discover a range of other homemade delights.
★ **Animal bonding** Make new furry friends and spend some quality time with the sheep of Gozo.

Practical details

Your private Gozo shepherd experience is bookable via **Gunyah** (gunyah.com, click on Malta and 'Cultural Heritage Breaks'), and includes transfers to/from Malta, overnight accommodation and the first day to explore Gozo at your own pace. The required overnight stay ensures early-morning arrival on the farm.

Other options

Turophiles (cheese-lovers) have a wide range of cheese-making workshops to choose from all across the globe, many using raw milk and some located on farms. As an example, you can meet a Sicilian shepherd through the **Association for Tourist Services Culture and Environment** (supramonte.it) in Orgosolo, spending a day with a *pastore* and helping him prepare his local cheese.

Doing it at home

Impress your foodie friends with a whiff of the Mediterranean. Check that you've got all the right hardware, especially cheese moulds (available online). If you can source raw sheep's milk, do so, although unpasteurised, full-fat cow milk will serve in a pinch. Serve with ħobża if you can find it – it's a truly amazing crusty sourdough bread.

After all the fun and hard work it's time to taste if your cheese makes the Gozo grade.

ROLL YOUR OWN
CIGARS IN CUBA

Duration One day ✳ **Cost** £149 for two ✳ **Outcome** Delicate fingers, manual dexterity and an instant Groucho Marx prop ✳ **Where** Viñales and Vuelta Abajo, Cuba

Havana's Upmann cigar factory is a beacon to smokers serious about their habanos.

Pick, pack and roll leathery leaves under the tuition of a dedicated *torcedor* (cigar roller) in Cuba's cigar heartland.

WHAT TO EXPECT

To the rookie roller, crafting a few tobacco leaves into one of the world's most highly prized luxury goods might seem just a small step up from putting together a saggy student rollie. Think again. Creating a Cuban cigar – with a few nips and tucks – is the puffing industry's equivalent of face-lift surgery.

The pressure's on as soon as you get seated at the rolling station, surrounded by the paraphernalia of a pro: filler leaves, binder leaves, wrapper leaves, moulds, a guillotine, natural gum and metal blades. Nicotine novices get shown how to whip out a leaf's central vein in a single stripping action by wrapping the vein over their hand. Then the rolling begins.

Much like on TV cookery programs, stacks of cured and classified leaves have been prepared earlier, so all you'll need to focus on is rolling an arch-perfect cigar. Rolling is done at an angle, keeping the single leaf taut ahead of the roll; it's difficult to keep this even, as it can feel a bit like smoothing over a giant slug. And if you haven't mastered a seamless wrap, you'll have to start again – after all, this is what the buying punter will see as the final smoke in the cedar box.

Unfortunately, this isn't the end of the process as the cigars are then aged for a minimum of three years, so if you want to light up immediately you'll be puffing on someone else's hand-rolled creation.

How it suits you

The experience would most appeal to the cigar connoisseur, and to DIY and artistic types curious about the age-old technique. A large dollop of patience and delicate hands are required – fumble-fingered folk need not apply.

What you'll get from it

★ **Method** There's no making it up as you go along, unless you think you've mastered in a day what Cuban apprentices take at least a year to grasp.

★ **Know-how** You'll savour your smokes even more after crafting the humble Cuban leaf from scratch and knowing how Cuban farmers have to care for the 'devil's grass' for nine months a year.

★ **Kudos** Take your batch of *habanos* home (unless you're a US citizen). Bringing an own-made souvenir back home surely ranks high among top holiday experiences!

Practical details

Esencia Experiences (esenciaexperiences.com) offers tours of plantations and cigar-rolling lessons in Vuelta Abajo, western Cuba, where the best tobacco leaves in the world are grown. To see the tobacco plants in full flourish, visit the region between December and March.

Other options

Head to the Bahamas for classes at **Graycliff** (graycliff. com), whose original cigar blend was created by Avelino Lara, Fidel Castro's personal roller. **Exquisite Experiences** (exquisite-experiences.com), based in London, offers one-day classes.

Doing it at home

Unless you're going to train as a *torcedor* in Cuba, which could take up to four years, invite fellow cigar aficionados over for a stogie party. You could even don green fatigues and caps, the garb of Fidel Castro's 1959 Revolution rebels, to add an authentic flavour to the Cuban light up.

HANG TEN AT HAWAIIAN SURF CLASS

Duration Five days ✳ **Cost** From US$740 ✳ **Outcome** Greater focus, a sense of mastery and a burning desire to relocate to the beach ✳ **Where** Lahaina, Maui, Hawaii

WHAT TO EXPECT

With your board under your arm and your face kissed by the sun (sun block essential!), the warm water licks your feet as you slosh into the Pacific to catch another wave – your hair's barely wet but your coolness quotient has already gone up a notch. You're stoked ... why did you remain a passive observer of the ocean for so long?

Tahitians may have invented surfing, but it's the Hawaiians who've claimed this physical yet extremely spiritual pastime as their own. Hawaii was the first island culture to popularise surfing and to experiment with equipment and techniques, and its surfers ensured sacred rituals and prayers were incanted before any trees were cut down to make the boards (royalty had the longest!) and before anyone entered the ocean.

Now you, too, are feeling at one with the universe after you've mastered the practical stuff. You now know how to paddle out on your board, and that standing up is as easy as 1-2-3. You're also reminded that timing is everything in life and this is definitely the case with surfing – it's almost guaranteed you'll be standing upright on that board and riding a wave on your first day.

And having started off with ocean fundamentals, you've now got a better understanding of this watery element of Mother Earth: the tides, swells and currents and how to work with them, not against them.

How it suits you

For the adventurous traveller, surfing may already be on your bucket list of sports to try. If so, you'll most likely want to book a longer course so you can graduate to bigger waves and max out on the experience. Spontaneous travellers will take to surfing like a fish to water, because it's all about going with the flow to keep your balance along the way. If you can't stand up the first few tries, you'll roll with it: you know you'll be hanging ten in no time!

What you'll get from it

★ **Exhilaration** Once you can catch a wave and ride on water, your natural endorphins will be cranked. This is something you'd do every day ... if only you could.

★ **Relaxation** You'll be having rip-roaring fun, but how about the Zen rush afterwards? Now you know why Hawaiians are so laid-back: it's something about the water.

★ **Body confidence** It takes a certain amount of strength and muscle tone to swim out in the ocean and maintain your balance on the board. If you're doing this every day, you can't help but tone up!

Practical details

Maui Surf Clinics (mauisurfclinics.com) offers surfing lessons all year long, but it's essential to book ahead. The school can recommend accommodation options.

Other options

Aussies can learn to surf at **Manly Surf School** (manlysurfschool.com). In Devon in the UK, **Surf South West** (surfsouthwest.com) offers lessons at Croyde and Saunton from late March to mid-November. **Learn to Surf LA** (learntosurfla.com) runs courses at iconic Malibu or Santa Monica, and other US locations. If you're in Portugal, try a surf camp at **Atlantic Riders** (atlanticriders.com).

Doing it at home

Transfer your surfing skills to land and get a skateboard or give snowboarding a try – it works on similar principles, with a few essential costume changes. Or grab some printed shirts and leis and host a Hawaiian theme party.

The ancient Hawaiian kings practised it here and you can too: could there be any better place to learn surfing than the warm, tropical waters that legendary surfer Duke Kahanamoku called home? *Aloha*!

Surfing is as much about learning respect for the ocean as it is learning new skills.

Don't feed the animals: Churchill is the polar-bear viewing capital.

PERUSE POLAR BEARS IN MANITOBA

Duration Five days ✳ **Cost** C$5000 to C$5650 ✳ **Outcome** Tundra polar bear sightings, a naturalists' education on all things polar bear and an awareness of their plight ✳ **Where** Churchill, Manitoba, Canada

WHAT TO EXPECT

Want to see male polar bears fighting each other with club-sized paws? Mothers leading their young in a line across the frozen landscape? Cute-beyond-belief cubs toying with each other in the snow? Get yourself to Churchill, Manitoba, to learn the ins and outs of safely viewing these beautiful but potentially deadly life-size teddy bears.

There are no roads to the tiny seaport town of Churchill. After a two-hour charter flight from Winnipeg, you touch down on an icy tarmac in a blip of a town where polar bear warning signs are more common than stop signs. Remote enough for you? Wait, there's more.

The main action happens 16km out of town on the tundra, a permafrost landscape of muddy peat bogs and frozen ponds, whipped by Arctic winds. During October and November, the bears congregate here while they wait for Hudson Bay to freeze up so they can go hunting for ringed seal. This is your chance to watch the action from the protective warmth of purpose-built tundra buggies, which are designed to help protect the delicate ecology while keeping you out of harm's way.

When not on the tundra, the Eskimo Museum and dog-sledding expeditions offer insights into the local Inuit people, while the Parks Canada Interpretive Centre will further whet your appetite for natural and historical information, with tips for wildlife watching.

At night, keep an eye out for the aurora borealis and an ear out for bear warning shots – both are common after dark.

How it suits you

The remote location, extreme weather conditions and element of danger make this experience ideal for intrepid and adventurous personalities. It could also suit hermit types who can revel in the rawness of the environment. If you're a people person, Churchill's bubbly personalities have all the quirks of itinerant seasonal employees in a tiny town. They'll make you feel at home.

What you'll get from it

★ **Naturalist 101** Expert guides, slide nights and lectures mean imbibing all there is to know about polar bears.
★ **Chill factor** Keeping warm is all part of the experience. Temperatures on the tundra range between -5°C and -20°C, and -40°C when the wind blows.
★ **Indigenous digest** Lessons in Inuit lifestyle are a bonus.
★ **Photography** Tundra buggy time means brushing up on wildlife photography skills.
★ **Exclusivity** Visitors to the tundra need to be part of a tour group. Numbers are very limited and bookings need to be made nine months in advance, so consider yourself privileged.

Practical details

Frontiers North Adventures' (tundrabuggy.com) Churchill Town and Tundra Experience operates during October and December. Churchill is known as the 'polar bear capital of the world' and sightings are guaranteed.

Other options

Check out the **Great Canadian Travel Company** (greatcanadiantravel.com) for the chance of a bear sighting in Norway. In Greenland, contact **Nordic Visitor** (nordicvisitor.com).

Doing it at home

Frontiers North guests receive a one-year membership to **Polar Bears International** (polarbearsinternational.org) after visiting Churchill. Use your newfound knowledge to enlighten others on the plight of the polar bears. Have a slide night to raise funds for further research and education. Or simply wear a PBI T-shirt!

If you're a wannabe David Attenborough, intrigued by north Canada's enigmatic cold-climate critters, get up-close-and-personal with the ultimate polar bear 101.

SNIFF OUT A SCENT
AT PERFUME SCHOOL

Duration One- and two-week courses ✳ **Cost** €1200 to €1900 ✳ **Outcome** A discerning nose and a 'signature scent' that doesn't have somebody else's name on it ✳ **Where** Provence, France

How it suits you

Exposed to a seemingly endless range of scents, emotional types are amazed at the impact each perfume can have on their state of mind. It's like playing with some kind of magic. If you're into history, you'll be steeped in the past as you wander the narrow streets of Grasse, explore the link between flower cultivation and natural perfume-making, and begin to understand the evolution of a profession that is tied firmly to this medieval town.

What you'll get from it

★ **Intuition** There's a heavy dose of science in perfumery, but with so many elements to choose from it's not completely objective … you'll literally be following your nose and going with your gut.
★ **Appreciation** After zooming through life at a million miles an hour, you'll remember how pleasant it can be when you stop and smell the roses.
★ **Mindfulness** Now that you've taken the time to focus on the development and enjoyment of just one of your senses, you're ready to enliven the others. Next stop: wine and cheese tasting!

Practical details

Sign up for Fragrance Summer School at the **Grasse Institute of Perfumery** (prodarom.fr). Lunch is included in the cost of tuition. Also in Grasse, the ancient perfume house **Molinard** (molinard.com) runs short workshops for visitors.

Other options

Try courses at the **Cotswold Perfumery** (cotswold-perfumery.co.uk) in the UK or **Fleurage** (fleurage-natural-perfume.com.au) in Melbourne, Australia.

Doing it at home

Those racks of essential oils at your health food store are not such a mystery any more: select a few and experiment to blend a spellbinding new scent. Or explore aromatherapy and learn more about the incredible powers of botanicals.

WHAT TO EXPECT

Leave glamorous Cannes behind and step into a storybook life at a perfume school in picturesque Grasse, the French cradle of perfume since the 18th century. Two-thirds of France's perfume production takes place in this gorgeous hilltop town, whose sunny climate and fertile soils are tailor-made for flower cultivation.

A spritz of your usual scent and you're off to join your classmates in an early-

Embark on a unique kind of French immersion by exploring the world of fragrance in Grasse, the centre of French perfumery for over 150 years.

20th-century Provencal house, where the production cycle behind your favourite perfumes is about to be demystified. You're also about to learn how the craft has evolved through the ages, incorporating synthetic as well as natural components.

Along the way you'll acquire an esoteric vocabulary, as professional perfumers escort you on a sensory journey through the top, middle and base notes that combine to make a classic perfume. One moment you're thinking about the molecular components of fragrance, asking about chemical concepts like solubility and volatility; the next you're training your nose in the workshop, 'playing' at the perfumer's organ, which comprises hundreds of tiny bottles of essences.

Summer school was never this heavenly, as you take field trips to local flower-growers and experience resplendent lavender, tuberose and jasmine plantations in full bloom. With dozens of components used to make single perfumes and over 500 raw materials to work with, your head and heart are duly inspired to blend an intoxicating fragrance you can call your own.

The scent from lavender fields wafts over Provence in the summer.

DIG INTO HISTORY IN ISRAEL

Duration Two to seven weeks ✳ **Cost** From US$400 per week ✳ **Outcome** Dirt under your fingernails, Indiana Jones insights and a hands-on look at history ✳ **Where** Tel Megiddo, Israel

WHAT TO EXPECT

You wake up at the crack of dawn at Tel Megiddo (known as Armageddon in the New Testament), and spend the day sweating over ancient rubble. And when you crawl into bed long after dark, you're dreaming of doing it all over again the next day. Such is life on an archaeological dig in Israel.

Work starts at 5am to beat the unrelenting Middle Eastern sun. Shaded by a tarp, you methodically uncover layers of dirt and – hopefully – artefacts that were last seen by human eyes a hundred generations ago. Sometimes you swing a pickaxe like a gravedigger, at others you wield tools so tiny you feel like a dentist, but the goal is always the same: to learn about ancient civilisations through the objects they left behind.

At least as important as the artefacts themselves – potsherds, stone tools, the occasional oil lamp or bone – is the context in which they were found. What else was buried in the same layer? That burnt organic material – can it be attributed to a specific historical event, like a battle? As you work, you'll learn how archaeologists – like forensic investigators at a very cold crime scene – record every scrap of information that might shed light on what happened long, long ago.

How it suits you

Unearthing the past is likely to appeal to people who are really into history – after all, at an archaeological dig you encounter the past at its most immediate and raw. The discipline of recording every possible detail about finds would be most appealing to people who, by nature, are organised. On the other hand, you never know what lies beneath your next spadeful of earth: most likely more dirt, but possibly an ancient coin or even an inscription. So it's important that you can go with the flow, able to deal with routine but prepared at all times for a 'eureka' moment.

What you'll get from it

★ **Meet our ancestors** The closest thing to travelling back in time and introducing yourself to the ancients.
★ **Immediacy** Brushing away dirt to reveal an ancient bowl is a lot more exhilarating than watching an archaeology program on TV.
★ **Scholarship** You're an active participant in expanding our empirical knowledge of the ancient past.
★ **Teamwork** Digging requires exquisite coordination between field archaeologists, forensic anthropologists, archaeozoologists, botanists and chemists.

Practical details

Most archaeological digs in Israel, including **Tel Megiddo** (megiddo.tau.ac.il), take place between mid-May and August. For details, check out the websites of the **Biblical Archaeology Society** (digs.bib-arch.org/digs) and the **Israeli Foreign Ministry** (mfa.gov.il; see 'Archaeological Excavations' under 'Latest Releases').

Other options

Archaeological societies, found in many countries and all 50 US states, are a great source of information on local digs. Details on excavations around the world can be found on the **Archaeological Fieldwork Opportunities Bulletin** (archaeological.org/fieldwork/afob).

Doing it at home

For a children's birthday party, you could salt the sandbox with 'artefacts' and then have all the invitees – equipped with spoons and paintbrushes – participate in a 'dig', with a prize for whoever finds the Rosetta Stone! **Dig** (digonsite.com) has articles on archaeology for kids.

Around the time of King Solomon, a clay pot shatters amid the chaos of an Egyptian siege. The next human being to pick it up could be you!

King Herod's tomb in the Judean Desert wasn't discovered until 2007.

STRETCH YOURSELF IN INDIA'S YOGA CAPITAL

Duration Daily classes ✳ **Cost** Around 250 rupees per class ✳ **Outcome** An intimate physical knowledge of a centuries-old spiritual tradition – plus enviable flexiness ✳ **Where** Rishikesh, India

WHAT TO EXPECT

The enchanting little town of Rishikesh, in the foothills of the Himalayas, burst into Western consciousness in the 1960s when the Beatles visited to pay their respects to the Maharishi Mahesh Yogi. Ever since then the town has been a magnet for spiritual wanderers, developing into the 'yoga supermarket of India' with an ashram or school on every corner.

Don't let the hordes put you off. As well as attracting Western pilgrims, Rishikesh is an important destination for Hindus, who come to visit major temples on the holy River Ganges. It's a vibrant place with a palpable charge and a very real spiritual life.

Opinions on the origin of yoga differ, but it's agreed that India was its birthplace, and that it was developed partly by the *rishis* (mystic seers) after which Rishikesh is named. There's something pretty auspicious about following in their footsteps, kicking off or deepening a yoga practice here.

Most schools and ashrams offer daily classes, so you can shop around for a teacher and style that suit. Once you're into the swing of your routine, you'll be rewarded with benefits like improved posture, better sleep and digestion, and greater calm.

How it suits you

While you can approach yoga as a fitness activity, most serious practitioners – particularly in India – emphasise its spiritual component, the connections it forms between body, breath and mind. Spiritual types will relish the inner workout as much as the outer, and rational types might be in for a revelation. Social butterflies will enjoy yoga in Rishikesh – there are plenty of like-minded souls ready to swap aching-limbs stories over an ayurvedic tea.

What you'll get from it

★ **Reunion** In stressful Western lives, mind and body can tend to become estranged. Yoga is an excellent way of reintroducing them to each other.

★ **Communion** There's no better way to tune into the atmosphere of Rishikesh and its many spiritual communities than by embarking on a yoga mini-odyssey.

★ **A healthy dose of smug** Waking up in a beautiful place and fulfilling a commitment to the wellbeing of your body will make you high on life ... and just a little bit pleased with yourself.

Practical details

The **Omkarananda Ganga Sadan** (omkarananda-ashram. org) ashram specialises in Iyengar classes; try a seven- or 10-day course. The ashram holds a candlelit ceremony each night on the banks of the river.

Other options

Yoga options abound throughout the world. If you're interested in its evolution in India, you might like to try Ashtanga, one of the oldest forms of yoga – perhaps at a retreat in Australia's dreamily beautiful **Blue Mountains** (bluemountainsashtangayoga.com.au) or, if you like to balance a healthy lifestyle with a healthy amount of play, in **Ibiza** (ibizayoga.com).

Doing it at home

Yoga tends to be pretty addictive, and a surprising number of people who start out doing it for health or fitness end up becoming deeply involved with it, some even training as teachers. Could this be a new career direction?

Get some balance in your life by plugging into one of India's most powerful spiritual centres in the country where yoga was born.

India's *sadhus* may inspire you to practise your yoga poses.

HELP BUILD A HUT IN A
SENEGALESE VILLAGE

Duration Two days ✳ **Cost** €50 (not including transfers) ✳ **Outcome** Reroofing and other useful skills, refined communal instincts and animal know-how ✳ **Where** Thioffior, Senegal

Guided by Kaolack villagers, you will learn to see nature in a whole new light.

Trade your many skills for an overnight homestay in the Senegalese community of Thioffior, about as far off the tourist track as you can get.

WHAT TO EXPECT

Ever wanted to learn how to reroof a hut in a remote Senegalese village? Well, here's your chance. In the Kaolack region of Senegal, about 200km east of Dakar, the residents of Thioffior village have grouped together to welcome *gans* (Wolof for 'foreigners' and 'guests') to their community and spend a couple of days helping out in the village.

When Waly Diouf organised a village stay for family friends, everyone saw how beneficial the exchange was for both invited guests and hosts. Since then the villagers have opened their homes to more visitors, who are encouraged to join in the everyday tasks at hand. These tasks might include fetching water, preparing meals, working in the fields, tending animals or building wood-stick fences.

A typical two-day, one-night stay has you following the locals' lead as they pace through the daily routine of the village. On your arrival, a reception committee presents you with a symbolic gift and encourages you to eat with a local family. Then a task is set for you from the locals' to-do list, and your village education begins.

If the traditional huts' hay roofs need attention, you join a group headed into the red-earth bush to gather raw materials. As part of a human chain that loads a cart, you become one with the surroundings – wet and green or dry and dusty, depending on the season, but always hot. After your group lugs the cart back to the village, you're then taught how to prepare the materials and secure them in place. And *voilà* – you've learnt how to reroof a hut. What's next?

How it suits you

You never know what needs doing in Thioffior, so it helps if you're a capable Mr or Ms Fix It type. You should be ready for anything – harvesting, repairs, livestock handling, cooking, clothes washing … Spontaneity is also an asset. If you have an altruistic streak, you'll enjoy knowing your money is helping improve village life.

What you'll get from it

★ **Reroofing skills** The perfect introduction to thatching a cottage, plus all manner of other skills, from water-fetching to handling goats.
★ **Fun charades** Visitors speaking Serere, Wolof, French and English will find some support, but it is up to you to take the initiative and communicate by any means possible directly with the villagers.
★ **Life experience** Working shoulder to shoulder with locals, and sleeping in a local house, you learn what matters most in the villagers' lives.

Practical details

Visits to Thioffior can be arranged at any time of year through **Saly Travel** (saly-travel.com; go to the Saly Accommodation page, then click 'Thioffior Village Group'). As the village is remote and hard to find, it is best to book with a transfer included.

Other options

For more ideas, see **Village Homestays** (villagehomestays .com), for village homestay projects across the globe. The **Zikra Initiative** (zikrainitiative.org) in Jordan allows you to celebrate the lifestyle and heritage of village life during an 'exchange tourism' experience. Or meet your inner *matai* (chief) with **Samoa Urban Adventures** (urbanadventures. com; see p162-163).

Doing it at home

Living like a village local in Senegal is an eye-opening experience, so why not try your hand at putting a hay roof on your kids' cubby house and inviting your friends to a Thioffior-inspired camp-out.

ICE FISH FOR YOUR SUPPER IN MINNESOTA

Duration An afternoon ✻ **Cost** Free ✻ **Outcome** The skills to catch your own food from under the ice, angling tips and a bunch of new friends ✻ **Where** Minnesota, US

Break the frozen surface of Minnesota's winter lakes and tap into a winter culture with Scandinavian roots.

WHAT TO EXPECT

Ah, Minnesota – the Land of 10,000 Lakes. The state's smooth scallops of water are home to such tasty fish as tuna and walleye, and summer isn't the only time for fisher types to snag a tasty meal. Thanks to a large population of residents with Scandinavian ancestry and an abundance of cold-blooded fish, ice fishing in Minnesota is a popular outdoor winter activity. It's a social and serene way to connect with the natural environment, catch some food and Zen out over an ice hole.

Minnesota's ice anglers usually erect small shelters to protect them from the wind and rain. Come winter, these ice shanties pop up like small cities on lakes where the fishing is good, and folks gather inside around the hole, staying warm, chatting and reeling in dinner. The vibe is lively, with parties and festivals held in these little 'shanty towns' throughout Minnesota's iciest months.

Ice fishing may seem simple at first, but there are skills to be learned. Besides knowing how to dress and whether the ice is safe, you'll need to learn how to use an auger to drill a hole, what kind of bait to use for specific fish and how to prepare your catch. Attend an ice-fishing workshop to bone up on the basics.

How it suits you

Hardy individualists will appreciate catching their own food in the harsh setting of a crisp winter day. If you are a hermit, you can make the experience as solitary as you like, spending a quiet weekend on the ice. The rational and organised will enjoy the methodology in drilling a hole, choosing bait and then filleting the catch. And if you love nature, ice fishing is a great way to be out in the wild during winter.

What you'll get from it

★ **A winter hobby** It's hard to get outside during the cold months, but ice fishing will give you a good reason to head out and breathe in the cold air.
★ **Sustenance** Teach someone to fish and you'll feed them for a lifetime. Now you can freeze, pickle, grill, fry or bake the fruits of your labours, and treat your friends and family.
★ **Patience** The process of ice fishing will hone your focus and patience, from understanding the ice and chopping or drilling a hole to waiting and watching for fish.

Practical details

The **Department of Natural Resources** (nps.gov) runs ice-fishing workshops through the winter in Minnesota, with bait, tackle and poles included as part of the deal.

Other options

In Europe, **Lapland Safari** (lapinsafarit.fi) takes winter travellers by snowmobile from the Finnish village of Saariselkä for a morning of ice fishing. Participants fry their fish around a campfire. In Canada, the landscape, climate and European heritage of Ontario are similar to Minnesota's, so ice fishing is also a popular wintertime sport. Hook up with **Lake of the Woods** (icefishlakeofthewoods.com) for a guided ice fishing trip.

Doing it at home

If you live in an icy climate, then congratulations: you have a fun new winter hobby! If you're from warmer climes, consider taking an alternative winter vacation: while folks head for beaches and palm trees, travel to the frozen water and keep warm inside cosy ice shanties.

Patience and the ability to tolerate icy cold is rewarded with a small fish.

CARVE A CANOE FROM A TREE TRUNK IN ESTONIA

Duration Six hours ✳ **Cost** Workshops from €70 ✳ **Outcome** Well-hewn muscles and membership of Europe's only dugout-canoe-building society ✳ **Where** Soomaa National Park, western Estonia

Build calluses while hefting an adze to help craft a dugout canoe, then relax on a paddle through Estonia's wildlife-filled wetlands.

WHAT TO EXPECT

Succumb to the hypnotic rhythm as you give shape to a traditional dugout canoe in western Estonia. This region is famous for its unique 'fifth season', or annual spring flood, a happily anticipated time of the year when boats are the best way to get around.

The most traditional vessel is the *haabja*, a dugout canoe formed from a single piece of aspen that can take a skilled craftsman up to three weeks to hew and bend into shape using handheld tools, brute force and fire. As part of this workshop, you can add your sinew to the carving effort, no ordinary task indeed.

Soomaa is the last and now only place in Europe where the culture of building and using dugout canoes has survived, preserving knowledge passed down through the centuries. Your workshop leader can proudly trace his skill lineage back through several generations of master builders. Before setting you the task of chipping away at a particular section of trunk with an adze, he'll share a brief history of dugout canoes in Estonia, from the Stone Age to the present, as well as his perspective on dugouts used on other continents.

A reinvigorating lunch is followed by a leisurely canoe trip on the waterway that's borne *haabja* dugouts through the ages, passing through swamplands teeming with wildlife.

How it suits you

The several hours of physical exertion – with an adze on land and a paddle on the water – make this experience best suited to an adventurer comfortable in the outdoors. A DIY-er handy with tools will definitely delight in the *haabja*-construction process. *Haabjas* are less stable than regular canoes, but anyone with river experience will quickly adapt; novices may be challenged.

What you'll get from it

★ **Cultural insight** By wielding an adze and a paddle, you become part of a powerful cultural tradition linking ancient boats with the distinctive Estonian natural environment.
★ **Nature appreciation** Soomaa National Park is a vast wilderness area of untouched peat bogs, rivers, flood-plain meadows and forests.
★ **Old customs** As recently as 1996, only two old men were able to build *haabjas*. By participating in this workshop, you'll help promote and preserve an endangered ancient practice.

Practical details

Haabja-building workshops are conducted from May through August by **Wilderness Experience in Estonia** (Soomaa.com). Check the website for details of one-on-one workshops and classes for up to four people. Transfers from Pärnu are possible by prior arrangement.

Other options

Across North America there's a revival in traditional skin-on-frame kayak building, with schools offering classes in different designs. In Bolivia, in the village of **Huatajata** (thepachamamaproject.blogspot.com.au) on the shores of Lake Titicaca, the world's first reed-boat building school has on staff a guy who helped shape Thor Heyerdahl's vessels.

Doing it at home

With yard space, the right size tree trunk and an adze, you could make this a home project to chip away at over a very long time. More reasonably, apply your newfound canoe-handling skills on a local river. It's an ideal, low-impact way to stay physically and mentally fit, and a nature-friendly way to remember your ancient forebears' history.

If the canoe-makers know their stuff, you won't need those lifejackets.

HEAD FOR THE HEIGHTS IN THE LAKE DISTRICT

Duration One day ✱ **Cost** From £95 ✱ **Outcome** Fitness, fearlessness and agility – you'll be a rock star (only without the screaming fans) ✱ **Where** Kendal, England

How it suits you

Rock climbing satisfies the adrenalin-rush appetite of the most adventurous of travellers. You don't have to be particularly fit or strong: as beginners, women often have better technique than men because they use their legs more than their arms. It will appeal to lateral thinkers who will enjoy figuring out their way to the top of a climb; sometimes you have to go sideways to go up. And those who relish a challenge will be eager to progress to harder grades of routes.

What you'll get from it

★ **Self-confidence** Gaining the confidence in your own abilities to lead a pitch is invaluable; there's nothing like facing and overcoming your fears to put a spring in your step.

★ **Problem-solving** Sometimes the obvious way is not the best way, grasshopper.

★ **Safety skills** You'll learn how to tie into a harness, use ropes, and read the rock and the weather conditions – handy skills to have up your sleeve for who knows what other occasions.

Practical details

The **Lakeland Climbing Centre** (kendalwall.co.uk) is a good starting point, with courses introducing beginners to outdoor climbing and refresher sessions for more experienced climbers. May to October is the prime climbing season; you can practise your moves on the centre's 18-metre indoor wall during inclement weather.

Other options

The rock formations of Joshua Tree National Park in southern California attract novice and expert climbers from all over the world; local climbing schools help you up some of the 8000 routes. At its Blue Mountains base of Katoomba, the **Australian School of Mountaineering** (climbingadventures.com.au) offers introductory and advanced rock climbing programs.

Doing it at home

Sign up at your local indoor wall-climbing centre to perfect your moves. Outside, your climber's eyes will scan cliffs – even in urban areas – for routes. The downside? Your knowledge of knots and safety rope techniques means you'll be the natural go-to person for friends and neighbours with chimney troubles.

WHAT TO EXPECT

'Elvis Leg', getting 'belayed' but hopefully not having 'a screamer': these are all terms you'll encounter as you gain a head for heights on a rock-climbing course in the Lake District.

Elvis Leg is the uncontrollable shaking of your leg as your ponder your next move. A belayer is your trusted companion paying out the safety rope at

Your fingertips stretch for the slightest of holds. Your rubber shoes are smeared onto the rock face and the only way out is up. Where better to connect with rock climbing's gritty roots than its crucible, England's Lake District?

the foot of the climb; a screamer is when that rope is tested with an extra-long fall. In the experienced hands of your instructor, however, that's a highly unlikely possibility.

The Lake District – a northwestern landscape of crags, ridges too rugged to be labelled hills and, yes, lots of lakes – was the birthplace of recreational rock climbing.

It was here that the Romantic poet Samuel Taylor Coleridge experienced that compelling combination of fear and pleasure while scaling Scafell in 1802. But it wasn't until 1886, when Walter Haskett Smith summited Napes Needle, a stone spire in the heart of the Lake District, that rock climbing really came of age.

Haskett Smith climbed without

ropes but your introduction to the activity will focus on safety: how to use a harness, ropes, knots and belayers, and the dos and don'ts of clipping in and out of karabiners.

Rather than tear your eyes away from scouring the rock for your next handhold, wait until the top of your first climb to appreciate some of England's most breathtaking views.

Use your new Spiderman skills to capture views like this one, overlooking Wasdale Head.

Prepare to learn make-up, perfect poise and how to make it as your femmeself.

CROSS-DRESS FOR
SUCCESS IN NEW YORK

Duration 2.5 hours to two days ✳ **Cost** From US$450 ✳ **Outcome** Strengthen your femme side, and take a crash course in social etiquette ✳ **Where** New York City, US

WHAT TO EXPECT

The world's first transgender 'finishing school for boys who want to be girls' matches cross-dressing with classic etiquette lessons, but in an enjoyable way. Even the enrolment form tells you to have fun: what kind of female side do you have? Sissy maid? Mommy's little girl? Pregnant? Sophisticated career woman? Or maybe you are a 'cross-dressing virgin' looking for help.

With the motto to let your 'femmeself' open you up to the world, this is not mere drag or impersonation. Here the performance space you are prepping for might be an everyday scenario – dining at a restaurant in the Big Apple or pouring tea as a servant girl. The more you let your femmeself out, the happier and healthier you'll be, says the academy.

While you're getting ready for your debut, let yourself be pampered in the live-in dorm, taking a female sexual energy class. Then be guided through the right clothes, wigs and makeup to build your inner-female's confidence and put your best heel forward, all in private one-on-one classes.

Even biofemmes need lessons on how to pose, sit and walk in vertigo-inducing shoes, so walking classes are open to lady-born ladies too. The trick to heels, it seems, is to take long strides.

Soon you'll be showing off your new femme skills to the city, maybe with your wife by your side, if she hasn't already been alongside you the whole time. Yes, partners are allowed to accompany you to the academy – this is New York after all.

How it suits you

For the intrepid traveller, the wildest terrain to explore may yet be the hidden inner space of your identity. Social butterflies will love how much more fun they can have as a blonde. Or a brunette. And a bit of fun in a frock never hurt anybody, especially spontaneous travellers. In a city with a million different faces, trying a new one on will bring you closer to being a true New Yorker.

What you'll get from it

★ **Confidence** Stepping out in heels as your femmeself from a yellow cab to a glitzy restaurant will turn heads and you'll love it, knowing you have arrived in *the* city.
★ **Freedom** There are some things that only your femmeself will let you say, do or feel.
★ **Equilibrium** Everybody has a feminine side, and this will just bring it into balance.
★ **Poise** Refined movements can bring a level-headed coolness to anything you do.

Practical details

All clothes and accessories are provided at **Miss Vera's Finishing School for Boys Who Want to be Girls** (missvera.com) in New York City. Even better, classes can be conducted under a pseudonym.

Other options

Cabaret Floridita's Drag Queen Dance Classes (floriditalondon.com) in London teach all women how to walk in heels and dance to a Beyoncé song in 'drag'. In Milan, **Nina's Drag Queens** (www.atirteatro.it, in Italian) is a school aimed at actors and those who want to make drag their profession.

Doing it at home

Now that you've learned to walk and talk with olde-world charm, you may want to go on to spend more time sashaying in heels. But you don't have to. The modern man can move with grace and yet still be masculine, bringing the agility and fluidity of a sports hero to his manself.

Strut your inner female and expand your fabulous empire state of mind at a cross-dressing academy for boys who want to be girls.

ROCK OUT ON THE SITAR IN INDIA

Duration Two weeks ✳ **Cost** From 14,600 rupess ✳ **Outcome** Unlock hidden creative depths and head home with an enviable musical repertoire ✳ **Where** Delhi, India

WHAT TO EXPECT

It's easy to be overwhelmed by your first encounter with a sitar – the number of tuning pegs running along the length of its neck is truly alarming. But slip a *mizrab* (wire plectrum) onto the forefinger of one hand and draw it across the strings, and it's easy to coax rich sounds from this vibrant instrument.

That's not to say that your first raga will come quickly. While Western music has a dozen semitones to the octave, Indian classical music has 22 intervals known as *shrutis*, which give each raga its deep complexity.

It'll help if you're familiar with doh, re, mi ... but Indian music works with sa, re, ga, ma, pa, dha, ni, sa, and each note is unmistakably resonant, thanks to the sitar's combination of drone and sympathetic strings.

To play the sitar, you'll sit cross-legged and serene in your guru's studio while the heat and bustle of India builds to a crescendo outside. You'll discover melody lines on the top strings, and that the arched wire frets are placed to deliver the right notes. This makes life much easier when you start to improvise each raga.

And when you've spent a long day getting your head around the *tala* (the Indian system of rhythm) or bending strings to coax subtle microtones from your instrument, you'll head out onto the streets to immerse yourself in music from Bollywood movies to classical performances featuring players of the highest calibre.

How it suits you

Developing a repertoire of ragas will enrich the musical traveller's approach to any instrument. Culture seekers will appreciate discovering the full complexity of Indian music, finding themselves part of an ancient chain of musical knowledge, passed from teacher (guru) to student (*shishya*) over hundreds of years.

What you'll get from it

★ **Spiritual calm** You'll need to devote hours of almost meditative practice to make real progress.
★ **Musicality** Learning an ancient musical art form like this will enhance the way you listen to music or play any instrument.
★ **Culture** This experience will deepen your understanding of India in a way that a trip to the Taj Mahal never could.
★ **Party piece** No matter how poor your grasp of ragas, the fact that you can pick up and play an instrument like this will impress for years to come.

Practical details

It's easy to hook up with a sitar teacher in cities across India, but it's a good idea to organise lessons before you go. Delhi-based **Sanjeeb Sircar** (sanjeebsircar.com) is an award-winning performer and tutor.

Other options

Check out the **London Sitar Academy** (londonsitaracademy. co.uk) in the UK, or look for a similar group in your own country. If you want to find sitar teachers around the world, check out **Chandra & David's** (chandrakantha.com) website, with tutors listed who are prepared to teach via Skype.

Doing it at home

If you already play the guitar, you can explore sitar-like sounds with a variety of alternative tunings. We found that down-tuning strings from EADGBE to BF♯BF♯BB worked well, with the lower strings delivering the drone so you can find your melody on the high B string. You'll find plenty of other tuning options and instructional videos online.

Explore the wonders of Indian music by getting your fingers around one of its most distinctive instruments, the sitar, and discover a new side to your musicality.

As a *shishya* of the sitar you follow in the steps of legendary maestro Ravi Shankar.

ROLL PASTA LIKE NONNA'S IN SOUTHERN ITALY

Duration One day to one week ✴ **Cost** €295 to €1700 ✴ **Outcome** Italian cooking skills, a preference for fresh pasta and lots of local flavour ✴ **Where** Lecce, Southern Italy

Make your Nonna proud – hit the kitchen, roll up your sleeves and start making pasta the traditional Italian way.

WHAT TO EXPECT

Jamie Oliver did it: travelling through Italy, learning how to make dishes the traditional way. While you might not have the TV budget or film crew following your every move, there's nothing stopping you from heading to Lecce on the heel of Italy for your own cooking class. The perfect setting for an authentic pasta-making class, Lecce has been dubbed the Florence of the south.

The Awaiting Table school here certainly ticks all the right boxes. Classes are held in a home-style kitchen built in an 18th-century building. There's everything from a wood-fired grill to hand-made racks for drying pasta, plus a wine cellar, of course (where you'll be feasting on the meals you've just whipped up).

A day course starts with an espresso or three, before a visit to the local markets to pick up produce. Then it's time to hit the kitchen, where you'll be taught how to make pasta from scratch. It could be gnocchi, ravioli, tagliatelle or simple spaghetti or fettuccini. You'll get the hang of it pretty quickly: after all, most pasta types are made with flour, eggs and lots of kneading.

Taste the fruits of your labour, then have a nap before heading out for a local tour. You'll then come back to prepare dinner (more pasta!). The local wine will keep the conversation flowing late into the night ... just try not to forget everything you've learnt.

How it suits you

Gourmet travellers will be immersing themselves in the best possible way. Lessons are taught by Italian chefs (in English, though Italian is a possibility if yours is up to the task), using local produce and following local techniques. For the cultural traveller, you'll be visiting a provincial town rich in history, and the class also incorporates local history into its itinerary.

What you'll get from it

★ **Method** Learn about ingredients and the proper way to put them all together to make the perfect, rustic pasta. You'll be able to tell the difference between that tubular pasta (penne) and that flat one (fettuccine).
★ **Awareness** No more clumsily bumbling around the kitchen. Learning how to make pasta from scratch like a nonna (grandmother) is just part of the fun – you'll also gain kitchen skills by crafting dishes with your homemade pasta.
★ **A dirty apron** Who says kneading dough isn't messy? Expect things to get dusty when you're working with flour.

Practical details

Book the course via the **Awaiting Table** (awaitingtable. com) website, then make your way to Lecce in Southern Italy. Week-long courses are also available. If you get bitten by the Italian cooking itch, find a list of other food courses at **Food & Wine** (foodandwine.com, search 'Italy's top cooking schools').

Other options

Head to Victoria's **Sorrento Cooking School** (sorrentocookingschool.com.au) in Australia for three-hour pasta-making lessons, or try **La Cucina Caldesi** (caldesi. com) in central London.

Doing it at home

Start small by preparing a special meal for your other half. When your confidence and skills improve, ring your family and friends and get them over for some rustic Italian fare. Of course, show your *nonna* that she's not the only one who can make authentic pasta. Stuck for gift ideas? Pasta makes a beautiful and very practical present.

Showing off your new pasta-making skills will be irresistible once you get home.

PAINT A LEOPARD ON
ART SAFARI IN MALAWI

Duration Two weeks ✱ **Cost** £3000 ✱ **Outcome** Panache with a paintbrush, confidence in your creativity – and the ability to recognise when an elephant's about to charge ✱ **Where** Malawi

If you're lucky enough to sketch a leopard in the wild you won't have time to count their spots.

Unleash your inner artist in one of Africa's most canvas-worthy corners: learn to sketch, scribble and paint the wildlife, while you're out among it.

WHAT TO EXPECT

First, what *not* to expect. You can forget still-life subjects, nine-to-five lessons or anything like a regular classroom. A Malawi art safari is not your conventional kind of schooling.

No, in this serene-and-smiling sliver of East Africa, the great outdoors is your studio. And it's great indeed – especially the gentle mopane woodlands and rich riverine plains of Liwonde National Park. Not as famed as the Serengeti, perhaps, but pretty as a picture – and teeming with life.

Liwonde is a place to melt into, not rush around. Which is why learning to paint here is so very appropriate. The discipline forces you to slow down; to sit still and let the park's profusion of wildlife come to you.

Lessons start early – before dawn in fact – and 5am wake-up calls from hadada ibis will ensure you're up and out with your easel for sun rise. At this time of day, the light is like candy-floss, a soft glow that it's your challenge to put down on paper – with a few pointers from your enthusiastic tutor.

Other tasks might include perching on termite mounds to scribble grazing sable, drawing hippos so that they don't look like logs, and being innovative when an elephant blocks your path to an intended viewpoint (tip: keep a safe distance and sketch the elephant instead).

Days are spontaneous, special and peppered with advice and encouragement. Evenings are spent reviewing your efforts in a cool, open-sided bar, G&T in hand – the best kind of 'exam'.

How it suits you

The artistic traveller will be in their element. This isn't about producing line-perfect studies of basking crocs, it's about reacting to wildlife in the wild – fast, representative, fun. When sketching on safari, every stroke is imbued with the sight, smell and feel of the bush. The spiritual traveller too will take much from this experience: time to pause and contemplate, and absorb the glory of nature. Chaotic, restless types may be frustrated by the lack of movement, the staying in one place, but it's only by relaxing into Liwonde that you truly see it.

What you'll get from it

★ **Artistry** Small-group tuition will improve the skills of even the most amateur of artists.

★ **Creativity** Once you've tried to draw a live-action flapping, swishing, harrumphing elephant, you won't worry so much about the little details – it's all about capturing the essence of the animal.

★ **Patience** What's the rush? Be at one with simply sitting, waiting for the wild world to come to you, or just enjoying (and painting) the here and now.

Practical details

Art Safari (artsafari.co.uk, click on 'destinations' and Malawi) runs two-week painting courses in Malawi, which visit Liwonde as well as Mt Mulanje and Lake Malawi. The best time to visit is during the dry season, May to November.

Other options

In the UK, join an art workshop at **London Zoo** (zsl.org) – this less-exotic environ is a great place to practise your painting skills. Learn to dot-paint the lizards and roos of the Australian Outback on an Aboriginal-run art course at Uluru, or sail to Antarctica to draw penguin rookeries and whale flukes from the deck of an expedition ship.

Doing it at home

Carry a sketchbook everywhere – just a small one that you can slip into your bag. When you see something that inspires, rather than take a photo, get out your pencil instead. It forces you to stop and engage, whether that be with a herd of wildebeest or a gnarly old tree in the middle of a field.

HANDLE HORSES EXPERTLY IN MONGOLIA

Duration 10 days ✳ **Cost** NZ$2200 ✳ **Outcome** Learn to ride a horse like a Mongol, gallop through an untouched wilderness and experience an ancient culture ✳ **Where** Zavkhan, Mongolia

How it suits you

Group trips are the perfect social setting for do-ers, altruistic types and leaders. You'll be setting up and striking camp, and doing your share of the cooking, dishes and horse work. Butchering the mutton meat for dinner, for example, could be right up your Genghis Khan! Spontaneous types will relish the seemingly aimless itinerary, as will the intrepid adventurers.

What you'll get from it

★ **Saddle skills** Take a hint from the old adage: A Mongol without a horse is like a bird without the wings. There's no better place on earth to brush up on your horse and saddle skill set than here.

★ **Cultural insights** The remote location ensures the locals are genuine and always willing to share cultural anecdotes. You'll return knowing your yaks from your yurts.

★ **Soul searching** There's nothing like a wilderness immersion to put you in touch with the natural world. Out here there's time to lose yourself – or find yourself – in nature.

Practical details

Zavkhan Trekking (zavkhan.co.uk), a Kiwi–Mongolian partnership, operates several tours, including one through Afghanistan, departing each year between June and September. The 'Zavkahn Taster' trip is a shorter version of the 17-day Zavkhan Classic.

Other options

Equestrian Escapes (equestrian-escapes.com) organises horse tours in the UK and Europe. Australia's **High Country Horses** (www.highcountryhorses.com.au) has five-day horse adventures in the Victorian high country. In the US, **Equitours** (www. ridingtours.com) runs worldwide horse adventures including a seven-day 'Three Parks' spectacular in Arizona.

Doing it at home

Don't hang up your reins yet. With five days in the saddle under your belt, it's worth checking out local riding schools for information about leisure riding and horse rentals to keep up your skill level. Shorter horse tours and trail rides are also popular in many regional centres.

WHAT TO EXPECT

There are plenty of 'pony' rides to take near the capital Ulaanbaatar, but for a genuine horse adventure, on an unexplored track, you'll need to travel further afield to Zavkhan province. To get there, it's a ride in a small plane to Moron (that's right, Moron), followed by a challenging seven- or eight-hour drive. But it's worth it.

The Tarbagatai foothills are Lord of the

Ever dreamed of running wild on horseback, with the wind in your hair and a group of Mongolian tribesmen whooping encouragement in the background? No, it's not a nightmare – it's a dream come true!

Rings–style remote. You'll spend five and a half days in this landscape of dramatic mountains, forested hills and open steppe grasslands stretching to a far-off brilliant blue sky. With around six hours a day in the saddle, there's ample time to work on your horsemanship.

Mongol horses are a short, stocky breed, known for their calmness and sure-footing on tricky terrain –

ideal for the 25 per cent beginner adventurers on such a trip. With no fences and few trees, your steed is also perfect for picking up the pace. And whatever your ability, there are tips and techniques aplenty shared by the nomadic horsemen you meet along the way.

As they're quick to point out, horseriding is in the blood, and horses are an essential part of rural

life here. *Gers* (yurts), camels, yaks and sky-high eagles punctuate the scenery and make for perfect photo ops. At the end of each day, a couple of support vehicles provide creature comforts – tents, a camp oven, food and the occasional hot chocolate. Prepare to muck in – out here it's one-in all-in – and then, when dinner's done, sit back and enjoy that sunset.

Surefooted Mongolian horses are perfect for the wild terrain.

ROAST YOUR OWN COFFEE
BEANS IN GUATEMALA

Duration Four hours ✳ **Cost** From US$40 ✳ **Outcome** The know-how to outsmart a barista, Fair Trade insights and a caffeine jolt ✳ **Where** San Miguel Escobar, Antigua, Guatemala

Crunch coffee grinds in the Antiguan highlands with coffee farmers who'll show you how to pick, process and roast your own joe.

WHAT TO EXPECT

Learn about the effort involved in getting your brew to the breakfast table and you'll appreciate that cup of java all the more.

The small town of San Miguel Escobar is just 10 minutes from the highland city of Antigua, a top Guatemalan sight fabled for its gorgeous Spanish colonial architecture. San Miguel Escobar is unassuming, by contrast, but its economy is underpinned by small-scale independent growers and producers of some of the world's best – and most fairly traded – coffee.

To make the most of the Fair Trade brand cachet, a few of San Miguel Escobar's farmers are now offering visitors the opportunity to experience life on a coffee plantation for real.

Your private coffee experience starts in the fields, where, season permitting, you lend a hand picking the beans. Later, you learn how to sort and husk the coffee fruit, wash and ferment the beans, dry and remove the inner hull, sort again by size and grade, roast and – who could be denied it – taste the aromatic result. You might also learn why some farmers aren't entirely sold on whether Fair is all that fair ...

You'll also soon see that picking and producing coffee is no easy task: it involves long hard hours of work and a consistent devotion to quality.

How it suits you

When you visit San Miguel Escobar, you should be in a ready-to-do-it mood, keen to get into the hands-on mix. An inclination to be social and to go with the flow will make the experience that much more rewarding.

What you'll get from it

★ **Cultural insight** This immersive tour provides direct access to the insular but artisanal cottage-industry community of San Miguel Escobar.
★ **Community connection** Although a translator is present, direct interaction with locals is the norm, a way of witnessing firsthand how the coffee you drink is the farmers' economic mainstay.
★ **Warm glow** Your tour fee helps support local communities' efforts to grow sustainable businesses and improve living conditions.

Practical details

Your private Fair Trade coffee experience can be booked through **Gunyah** (gunyah.com, click on Guatemala and 'Cultural Heritage Breaks'). While the tour is available throughout the year, coffee picking is usually only possible between late November and mid-March.

Other options

While tours involving hands-on experiences are not commonplace, tours of Fair Trade coffee plantations are found in such countries including Costa Rica, Ethiopia, Guatemala, Mexico and Nicaragua. Tours of Fair Trade farms planted with chocolate, olives and fruit and nuts are also worth considering.

Doing it at home

Getting your hands on freshly picked coffee fruit can be quite a challenge, but acquiring green (unroasted) coffee beans isn't too hard. You won't be able to apply your new washing, fermenting, drying, hulling or sorting skills, but you can put your roasting prowess to the test.

Coffee lovers can follow the humble bean from field to cup.

EARN BEDOUIN CRED
AT CAMEL SCHOOL

Duration Two days ✳ **Cost** £190 ✳ **Outcome** Camel cowboy know-how and handy desert survival skills ✳ **Where** Wadi Freah, near St Katherine, Sinai, Egypt

You need to bond with your camel before you can work together as a team.

Learn the centuries-old camel-handling skills of the Bedouin on their turf, the vast and barren heartland of Egypt's Sinai Peninsula, and become a master camel-whisperer.

WHAT TO EXPECT

First things first: you need to hug your camel. Here, amid the forbidding sea of endless desert dunes, the dromedary is not just a pack animal but your vital friend and you're about to get up-close-and-personal with the Ship of the Desert.

Surrounded by the craggy claws of the Sinai High Mountains, you'll stay overnight at the camel school and spend time with the Bedouin who have lived in this harsh environment for centuries, adapting and shaping their lives around, rather than against it. For the Bedouin, the camel has played a fundamental role in their survival, and you'll learn a new respect for the desert and these hardy people who have made it their home.

From saddling and hobbling, crouching (getting a camel to sit down) and changing your camel's gait from *madd* (slow and rhythmic) to *sheiraad* (galloping dromedary-style; your first attempt is best compared to riding an out-of-control food blender), your patient Bedouin tutors will teach you the gentle command signals which turn these mammoth beasts into docile followers under your control.

At the start of the first day, you may struggle to mount your camel while it crouches. By the end of the second, you'll be equipped with the skills to lead your trusty desert companion and be jumping from the saddle, Bedouin-style, while your camel is still standing.

How it suits you

Man and beast pitted against the harshest of environments. What more could the swarthy adventurer want? Camel-handling ability is a must-do for any intrepid explorers who want to add desert survival skills to their bow. The more culturally inclined will enjoy this rare opportunity to interact with the Sinai's Bedouin, and to learn about their rich heritage and traditions.

What you'll get from it

★ **Confidence** The first time you manage to manoeuvre the bulk of your camel into a crouching position by simply making a soft 'shushing' noise will do wonders for your self-esteem.
★ **Patience** Working with animals requires persistence. You'll be learning from the Bedouin who, living within a climate of such harsh extremes, have grasped this deep level of calm.
★ **Slow travel** A 4WD may be quicker but nothing can beat the blissful ease of camel trekking. This style of travel allows the epic landscape to unfold languidly and envelop you totally, for you to be part of the scene rather than just a passerby.

Practical details

Wilderness Ventures Egypt (wilderness-ventures-egypt.com) runs camel-handling courses throughout the year at Muhammad Musa's Camel School. Book a camel trek with them afterwards to put your new-found skills into practice. Unless you're a sucker for sizzling heat, avoid the summer months of July and August.

Other options

Explore the Outback (austcamel.com.au) runs regular camel safaris in the Australian outback, where participants learn hands-on camel-handling skills. In Mongolia, the expansive Gobi Desert is a top choice for learning to ride Bactrian (two-humped) camels. And for a completely different location, **Joseph's Amazing Camels Company** (jacamels.co.uk) offers camel trekking in the wilds of Warwickshire.

Doing it at home

As it's not likely you'll find a friendly camel in your neighbourhood to show off your expertise, apply the Bedouin ability to work with, rather than against, their environment to day-to-day life. It's a talent we could all use.

WEAVE A NATIVE BASKET ON KODIAK ISLAND

Duration One month ✳ **Cost** US$30 donation ✳ **Outcome** Nimble fingers, patience and your own hand-woven basket in the Attu tradition ✳ **Where** Kodiak Island, Alaska

How it suits you

Detail-oriented crafters will appreciate the skill involved in weaving the basket and designing intricate patterns. The baskets' natural roots and utilitarian nature will please environmentalists, while history types will value the tradition of handing down skills from generation to generation.

What you'll get from it

★ **Weaving skills** Weaving containers from objects harvested from the natural environment may seem trivial, but it's a calming, quieting art form with a purpose: to carry things. Revel in its useful nature.

★ **Historical appreciation** Besides learning a skill, you'll join a tradition dating back thousands of years. You'll be taught by experts who were taught by other experts, and therefore become a part of the cultural lineage.

★ **Focus** You can't make patterns this tight and not pay attention. The repetitive work of weaving will also leave you with a sense of Zen, an almost relaxed focus that brings a centred feeling to your work.

Practical details

Kodiak Island's **Baranov Museum** (baranovmuseum.org) hosts a four- to six-week-long basket-weaving class every spring.

Other options

Basket weaving is a worldwide art, and opportunities abound in indigenous communities. In Australia, instructors at **Camp Coorong** (peaceliberation.tripod.com) teach Ngarrindjeri basket weaving to campers. Willow baskets are native to West Ireland, and since willow can only be harvested during the warmest six months of the year, the basket-weaving workshops operated by **Scoil Acla** (scoilacla.com), on Achill Island in County Mayo, begin after February's chill has thawed.

Doing it at home

With the right materials, there's no reason why you shouldn't be able to practise your weaving and eventually design your own patterns. These one-of-a-kind baskets make excellent gifts. Consider passing the tradition along by teaching a child the basic skills, or holding an informal workshop for neighbourhood kids.

WHAT TO EXPECT

If you think crocheting and knitting called for a tight weave, think again. In Attu, on Alaska's Aleutian chain of islands, the grass baskets are stitched up so tight they can even hold water.

Talk about getting back to basics: basket weaving is one of the world's oldest skills, an example of prehistoric

Learn about Alaska's rich native history while learning an ancient skill: basket weaving.

know-how that predates pottery and textiles. It's possible to weave just about anything fibrous, from thread and wood to straw, feathers and fur. Attu's fabric of choice has always been rye grass, which creates the island's especially finely woven baskets.

The Baranov Museum in Kodiak has been teaching Attu-style basket weaving since the 1950s, when an Aleut weaver began teaching this slowly dying skill. The teachers at the Baranov Museum were taught by her, so there is a direct lineage between an Elder expert and the skills you will learn.

The tone of the class often depends on students' interests (and the weather) – who wants to harvest grass when it's raining sideways? Because of the very tight weave, students make one small basket. Even for an expert weaver, it can take half an hour to weave one complete turn around an object as small as a soft-drink bottle.

Turquoise Lake: native Alaskans used baskets to carry resources around their awe-inspiring home.

RELEASE YOUR INNER CELT
IN SOUTH UIST

Duration Five days ✻ **Cost** £200 ✻ **Outcome** The skills to compose your own Gaelic ballad and play the music to go with it ✻ **Where** Daliburgh, South Uist, Scotland

An audience awaits your ballad to be sung across the wild *machair*.

Anyone with a dram of Scottish blood will feel the lure of learning the Gaelic language on a windswept Western Isle, with days of long vowels and nights of piping, fiddling and *ceilidhs*.

WHAT TO EXPECT

The odd shower is inevitable on these weather-beaten islands, but chances are you won't hear the rain over the driving pulse of the Highland pipes. Staying in a remote island community, you'll learn to speak Scottish Gaelic from people who never stopped speaking it, immersed in a world of windswept hillsides, silent lochs and white-sand beaches backed by rolling *machair* (wild meadows).

Your companions on this Gaelic journey will be a mix of far-flung Scottish expats and locals who can trace their family line back to Viking invaders and Pictish tribes. Spanning the generations, some will be gifted Gaelic speakers, others will be struggling with their first words, but a sense of shared history will run through the days like a Scottish reel. Think of it as a family reunion for relatives who haven't seen each other in generations.

Don't expect the Hollywood version of Scotland; in place of romantic castles, you'll find simple community halls and scattered farmhouses. But the traditional music of the isles will ring in your ears, from daytime classes in song, step dancing, piping and fiddling to living-room recitals and night-time *ceilidhs* with fiddle and pipe bands who raise the roof till the wee hours. You don't get that on the average language course ...

How it suits you

For some, studying Scottish culture in Scotland is an almost spiritual journey. Gregarious types will thrive on the atmosphere of cultural immersion, and a musical ear is a definite plus for song and dance classes. For Scottish history buffs, learning the language of their forefathers in the land they left behind is as close as you can get to time travel.

What you'll get from it

★ **Connection with the past** Even if your ancestors left Scotland centuries ago, this is a chance to rediscover your inner Celt.
★ **Inspiration** The beat of fiddles, pipes and voices holds a perfect mirror to the rhythms of life in the Hebrides.
★ **Cultural immersion** Song and dance aside, the experience of staying in a living Gaelic community is the real drawcard.
★ **Language skills** We're not saying you'll be fluent in a week, but Gaelic road signs and place names in the Western Isles will make a lot more sense!

Practical details

Gaelic courses abound on the west coast of Scotland, but **Ceolas** (www.ceolas.co.uk) has a musical string to its bow that transforms this from a language lesson into a full Celtic immersion. Courses on South Uist run annually in July. Most non-academic Gaelic courses run as summer schools, but if you're really keen you can find lessons year-round.

Other options

Learn Gaelic where the land runs out at **Taigh Dhonnchaidh** (www.taighdhonnchaidh.com), hidden at the northern tip of the Isle of Lewis. Practise your Gaelic vowels on weekdays, then test your comprehension at a Sunday sermon, when you study at **Lews Castle College** (www.lews.uhi.ac.uk) in Stornoway. Or spend a Gaelic summer at one of the great repositories of Gaelic knowledge, **Sabhal Mòr Ostaig** (www.smo.uhi.ac.uk) on the Isle of Skye.

Doing it at home

There are 25 million people with Scottish ancestry scattered across the globe, so you may be able to find someone to converse with in Gaelic just around the corner. Try contacting Scottish community groups and heritage organisations in your home town.

UNEARTH SHAMAN SKILLS IN THE AMAZON

Duration Two days to three months ✳ **Cost** US$700 to US$1100 per week ✳ **Outcome** Pick up herbal remedies and learn shamanic rituals ✳ **Where** Iquitos, Peru

Find out the features, foibles and functions of rainforest flora in the planet's most biodiverse location.

WHAT TO EXPECT

Forget about snapping pictures of crocodiles and monkeys in the rainforest. To really get to grips with the South American jungle, try wrapping your head around ethnobotanics, the study of the relationship between plants and people.

Iquitos, the Amazon's main ecotourism centre, offers several ethnobotanical learning experiences in the surrounding jungle, in gardens and atop jungle canopies.

At Cumaceba's Botanical Lodge you can explore an extensive garden with guides who'll explain the many uses of jungle plants, from treating HIV to protecting teeth from cavities. You'll even get to extract sugarcane juice from trees with the locals.

Up on the Río Napo, ExplorNapo Lodge has an garden filled with some 250 medicinal plants. The garden is curated by local shamans who offer explanatory tours, conduct healing ceremonies and guide visitors into the forest to find the garden's plants in their wild state (picking them from gardens is too easy for shamans). Take a walk on the nearby canopy walkway for a bird's-eye perspective on the mighty plant-life hereabouts.

You can further emulate the shaman's plant-embracing lifestyle by taking up Ashi Meraya Lodge's shamanic apprenticeships: you'll adopt the shaman's rainforest-plant-only diet and participate in trance-inducing ayahuasca ceremonies, with the aim of obtaining that ultimate level of chemistry with the jungle. Remember: the plant, so say all Amazonian shamans, is teacher.

How it suits you

Spiritually minded types should sign up now. If there is one Latin American experience designed to find the inner you, this would be it. But you'd better like roughing it with the shamans: accommodation will often be in basic huts.

What you'll get from it

★ **Perspective** Never again will you think that deforestation on the other side of the world is someone else's problem: you'll learn how we depend on Amazonian trees for 20 per cent of our oxygen and more besides.
★ **Tribal encounters** With the Amazon's indigenous population down to an estimated 200,000, opportunities for outsiders to have authentic contact are decreasing, but are still possible on these plant-focused learning curves.
★ **Health kick** You'll be able to decode the labels of health-food shop products after this (Amazonian cure-alls make up one in four ingredients used in Western medicine).

Practical details

The Amazon's best ethnobotanical experiences come courtesy of **Cumaceba Lodge** (cumaceba.com), **Explorama** (explorama.com) and **Ashi Meraya Lodge** (elmundomagico.org).

Other options

In the US, the University of Maryland's **Department of Plant Science & Landscape Architecture** (psla.umd.edu) gives students opportunities to study the plant life of exotic locales like New Zealand and Costa Rica. The UK charity **Plantlife** (plantlife.org.uk) has volunteer opportunities to learn about and protect plants at 23 reserves countrywide. In Australia, **Bushlore Australia** (bushloreaustralia.com.au) runs bush survival courses, including familiarisation with animals and plants.

Doing it at home

Those living in nontropical climes: don't despair. Amazonian plants can be nurtured as far north as Scotland. This is good news for those wishing to enhance their tropical plant knowledge closer to home, with public gardens like the UK's world-famous **Kew** (kew.org) offering year-round talks and home-growing tips on their exotic flora.

You'll learn something of the shaman's ability to identify the endless resources beneath the canopy.

POUR THE PERFECT
PISCO SOUR IN PERU

Duration Three hours ✳ **Cost** US$30 ✳ **Outcome** Market bartering skills, the perfect pisco-sour recipe and cocktail-pouring skills ✳ **Where** Lima, Peru

WHAT TO EXPECT

The pisco sour may not be as famous as Mexico's margarita, Cuba's mojito or Brazil's caipirinha, but it's just as potent a liquid cultural emblem, claimed by both Peru and Chile as their national drink.

Evidence points to a bar in Lima in the early 1920s as the elixir's place of origin, but both Peru and Chile dispute the other's boast of having invented the alcoholic brew. Such sociopolitical friction is all in a day's play, of course: Peru and Chile have a long history of sometimes bitter, or should we say sour (ouch!), antagonism.

Understanding this rivalry is just one part of what gets explored when learning how to make a 'real' pisco sour in Peru's capital, Lima. It's an education fitted to local interaction that includes a visit to Parque Kennedy in Lima's Miraflores neighbourhood, travel by *combi* buses to a market in nearby Surquillo, exploration of local products and exotic fruits (try a *camu camu, lucuma, granadilla* or *aguaymanto*), and then shopping. Every step of the way is a chance to chat with locals – especially when bartering in Spanish for pisco-sour ingredients.

The fitting finale is the preparation of the libation. Back in Miraflores, in a rooftop setting with gorgeous views of the coastline, you'll roll up your sleeves and, while tutored in the history and tradition of the pisco sour, squeeze your own limes and then blend the citrus juice with pisco brandy, syrup, egg white and ice. The final toast is a celebration of your newfound cocktail knowledge.

How it suits you

The task of absorbing pisco sour culture is best enjoyed by a go-with-the-flow person. Mixing and quaffing the drink is relaxing, but the rough and tumble of taking a *combi* (minibus) and negotiating prices with local merchants in Spanish requires spontaneity and spirit. Travellers keen on history will take particular interest in the background story of discord between Peru and Chile.

What you'll get from it

★ **Cultural insight** Drinking a pisco sour simply tantalises the taste buds, but putting it in its proper social context – understanding its complex history and culture – stirs the soul.
★ **Urban awareness** Most travellers avoid *combis* as the routes are often unclear and they contribute to Lima's urban bedlam. This trip demystifies *combis*, while raising awareness of some pretty serious urban planning issues.
★ **Local market zeal** Rubbing elbows with merchants and shoppers will cement your fondness for local markets.

Practical details

This pisco sour experience is offered through **Urban Adventures** (urbanadventures.com, click on Lima). Trips can be arranged throughout the year with 48 hours' notice.

Other options

Beer Tours (urbanadventures.com/beer_tours_around_the_world) are an increasingly popular evening escape, especially in cities with local craft brews and a whole lot of history. On a schnapps distillery tour in the Black Forest of Germany or the Zillertal region of Austria, you'll discover the traditions, raw materials and science of schnapps.

Doing it at home

At your next party, put your pisco-sour skills into practice. Explain the drink's contested history through a blind taste test that compares the Peruvian 'original' with its Chilean variant. Accompany it with a signature Peruvian ceviche.

From social trend to proper blend, sweeten your grasp of the sour in Lima and learn why Peru's most famous drink is a cultural force.

Spend time with the locals and soak up Lima's vibe if you want to put soul into your sour.

DIG FOR DINOSAURS IN PATAGONIA

Duration Two days ✳ **Cost** US$270 ✳ **Outcome** Unearth a creature that roamed the earth 200 million years ago and get in shape for *Jurassic Park IV* ✳ **Where** Neuquén, Patagonia, Argentina

How it suits you

For the anally retentive, details-obsessed person, this is as methodical as any work on the planet, using picks, awls, air scribes and even toothbrushes to slowly extract bones from the land in which they've lain for many millions of years. Into history? Dinosaurs might rule the pages of history books, but the idea of giant world-dominating lizards is almost unreal until that moment you uncover a piece of one beneath your feet.

What you'll get from it

★ **Method** This isn't like a dog digging for a bone, scratching and scrabbling at the earth. You must follow each painstaking step to ensure the preservation of the fossils.
★ **Precision** With 200 million years of natural history in your care, a steady brush hand is required.
★ **Imagination** That bone shard might once have been part of a giant dinosaur – it'll take a fair leap of the mind to picture it.
★ **Space to ponder** It's silent, solitary work, far from anywhere and anything, leaving the mind to wander not just through history but also life, the universe and everything in between.

Practical details

The **Centro Paleontológico Lago Barreales** (www. proyectodino.com.ar) is 90km northwest of Neuquén. Check the website for details about digs and tours.

Other options

In Australia, take part in the annual (February) dig at the **Dinosaur Dreaming** (dinosaurdreaming.monash.edu) site near Inverloch, Victoria. At Canada's **Dinosaur Provincial Park** (albertaparks.ca/dinosaur.aspx), bones lie scattered about like rubble, and you can head on to the nearby **Royal Tyrrell Museum** (tyrrellmuseum.com) to view its vast fossil collection. In the US, join a dinosaur dig in Fruita at the **Museum of Western Colorado** (museumofwesternco.com).

Doing it at home

With the skills you gain at Lago Barreales, the world is your dinosaur. Any likely bit of land can become the scene for some dino-exploration.

WHAT TO EXPECT

Even at the best of times, Patagonia can seem like a primeval place, rumbling with storms, its landscapes like something torn into shape by the teeth of a Tyrannosaurus rex. But it's when you look under the ground that things here get really interesting.

There are three major palaeontology sites around the city of Neuquén; more

Loved Jurassic Park? Fancy piecing together your own dinosaur skeleton? Make tracks to Patagonia to work with palaeontologists at one of the world's most important fossil beds.

dinosaur species have been found here than at any other place in the southern hemisphere. At the Centro Paleontológico Lago Barreales, it's possible not only to ogle bones but to work – as in get your hands dirty digging – on-site with palaeontologists in one of the world's only fully functioning dinosaur excavation sites open to the public.

Under the supervision of renowned palaeontologist and project director Jorge Calvo, you'll spend your days dusting off Cretaceous-period bones and picking at fossils, and your nights sleeping in the desert silence by the shores of Lago Barreales. It was around here that the bones of the world's largest-known dinosaur

(the 30m-long *Argentinosaurus huinculenis*) and the largest-known carnivore (the 8-tonne *Giganotosaurus carolinii*) were found, so a memorable dig is pretty much assured.

The other hundreds of finds include sauropods, dinosaur eggs, pterosaurs and prehistoric crocodiles.

Big foot: a sauropod's print by Lake El Chorón, Argentina.

FASHION A FLAMBOYANT
SARI IN JAIPUR

Duration One to two days ✳ **Cost** 800 rupees per day ✳ **Outcome** Carve a wooden block, create a design to rival Chanel or Warhol and print it on fabric ✳ **Where** Jaipur, Rajasthan, India

How it suits you

This course suits artistic types who want to create their own work of art, from carving their own design into the wood block to layering the colours printed onto the fabric. It also suits history buffs, who'll appreciate that this is an art form that has developed over many centuries. If you're into DIY, get ready to get hands-on.

What you'll get from it

★ **Serenity** The process of completing a pattern on a piece of a fabric is uniquely satisfying and soothing, as is the sense of learning a new yet ancient skill.

★ **Sleight of hand** There's a delicate precision to the block-printer's art.

★ **Insight** You'll gain a sense of how India's beautiful everyday artefacts are crafted, how the traditional artisans here work, and how the crafts have been passed down over generations.

Practical details

The **Anokhi Museum of Hand Printing** (www.anokhi. com) runs one- and two-day courses. It's around 20 minutes by taxi or rickshaw from Jaipur, which in turn is accessible by car or bus from Delhi and other places in Rajasthan.

Other options

At London's **CityLit** (citylit.ac.uk) you can take a four-week course in silkscreen and monoprinting. **Sydney Community College** (sydneycommunitycollege.com.au) in Australia offers seven-week hands-on courses, in which you can explore a variety of printing and colour techniques, and create your own designs on fabric.

Doing it at home

There are heaps of carved wooden blocks for sale at Jaipur's markets – buy a selection so you can create different patterns when you try out your new skills at home. Experiment with different fabrics and colours to create a range of effects.

WHAT TO EXPECT

Where better to learn the ancient skill of hand printing than the dusky pink city of Jaipur, one of India's major centres for the decorative arts, and the producer of hand-printed fabrics for centuries?

Jaipur seethes with bazaars full of exquisite patterned fabrics. These days many of these intricate patterns are created by machine, but the Anokhi

Learn the art of block printing from artisans whose skills have been honed over generations, then flaunt your own sari design in the bazaars of Rajasthan.

Museum seeks to keep the art of printing by hand alive via the use of carved wooden blocks. Housed in a terracotta-hued *haveli* (traditional house) that resembles a creamily iced cake, and centred around a courtyard, the museum lies on the edge of a sleepy village just outside Jaipur.

Head up to the museum's top floor, take your seat in a room slatted with golden sunlight, and learn the block-printing ropes from an experienced *chhippa* (block printer). You'll get to watch block carving in action, then learn how to carve your own block. Create your own design or choose a pattern from a book of designs.

Then you'll put your block to work to print a length of cloth, dipping it in brilliant colour then transferring it to the fabric. The deft *chhippa* will teach you how to layer print upon print to build up a pattern, one colour at a time, to create your own sari or fashion fabric.

Matching your block-print designs to the colourful array of fabrics is half the fun.

MASTER CHEESEMAKING IN CYPRUS' OLIVE GROVES

Duration From one day ✳ **Cost** €10 to €20 per day ✳ **Outcome** Handy cookery skills and an expanded waistline ✳ **Where** Büyükkonuk, North Cyprus

Seek out a pocket of tradition where the bread's fresh, the cheese is ripe and the olive oil runs free.

WHAT TO EXPECT

The north of severed Cyprus is the Turkish side, dotted with mosques, not churches, and where *hellim* (haloumi) is the cheese of choice, an unripened briny block of white deliciousness that's squeaky to the bite. If you fancy feta you need to cross the Green Line to the island's southern half, which belongs to Greece.

Even leaving politics aside for a second (which, hereabouts, is hard to do), this 'cheese-making' experience is about more than a dalliance with dairy. Stay in Büyükkonuk, the eco hub of North Cyprus, and you're buying into a whole – disappearing – way of life.

Büyükkonuk is a bulwark against the encroachment of mass tourism. Here, livestock, local gossip and backgammon boards rule; tourists in search of nightclubs and sun-loungers should look elsewhere.

Options are varied for the traveller willing to engage. There are donkey rides amid the olive groves, plus the chance to harvest those hanging green fruits, then squash out their oily loveliness at the communal press.

You could learn to knead vast loaves of bread flecked with sesame seeds, or milk a goat in the shade of a carob tree. Or you could stir a cauldron of curd to magic it into the region's salty speciality cheese. Finally, you could retire to the village square, to mingle with the residents and forget that the 21st century even exists.

How it suits you

Travellers with an eye for history will take as much from the politics outside their classroom as from the skills learned within it. Cyprus, an island split in two since 1974, is a fascinating example of history-in-action. Just let locals open the debate first. A trip here is not all about nations wrangling, however – it's about learning a new skill in a traditional setting (perfect for those hands-on do-ers). These skills are of the back-to-basics type: uncomplicated recipes and ancient chores that are perfect for calming the most chaotic traveller.

What you'll get from it

★ **Culinary nous** Show off to your friends by serving up homemade hand-squeezed cheese.
★ **Education** Get a Cypriot chatting over a glass of tea or some sheep udders and they're bound to start talking about Turkish–Greek relations.
★ **Simplification** Squint and you might believe you've travelled back in time, to when the clay oven and the millstone were the most important bits of kitchen kit; somehow things seem to taste that little bit better …

Practical details

Büyükkonuk eco-village sits in the foothills of the Besparmak Mountains. **Delcraft** (ecotourismcyprus.com) offers accommodation, cookery and village activity courses.

Other options

Stilton, Leicestershire's local cheese, takes time to make, so simply sample it for yourself in UK foodie hub Melton Mowbray. Or take a cheese course in Paris – learning how to select and serve various fromages, to most impress your guests – or forage for wild ingredients and fling in some feta on a cookery course on the Greek isle of Paros.

Doing it at home

You may not own an olive press but you most likely own an oven. Eschew those temptingly convenient readymade meals and make your dinners from scratch: it doesn't take that much effort, and tastes so much better. Cook basics on a school night, but challenge yourself with new recipes when catering for friends – the fun's in the experimentation.

Handmade halloumi:
learn traditional
techniques on Cyprus.

Mind & Body

BRUSH UP ON BUSHCRAFT
IN SOUTHERN AFRICA

Duration Two months to one year ✳ **Cost** Around 30,000 rand ✳ **Outcome** Learn about bushcraft and wildlife, and earn a recognised certificate in game ranging ✳ **Where** South Africa and Botswana

How it suits you

If walking with wildebeest sounds like too much adventure, this probably isn't the experience for you. But adventurous, practical travellers who relish the idea of hanging out with hyenas will be in their element. Game rangers by their nature are intrepid, can-do people – if that describes you, this could be the start of a whole new vocation.

What you'll get from it

★ **Bushcraft** Plug into the same skill-set that tribal people have been using to track wildlife around the savannah for, oh, about 200,000 years.
★ **Nature know-how** South Africa boasts 500 bird species and 300 different mammals; study hard if you want to sort your hartebeest from your kudu.
★ **Survival skills** Getting close to wildlife is one challenge; getting away without teeth marks in your rump is another!
★ **Accreditation** A level 1 field guide qualification is the first stepping stone towards becoming a wildlife pro.

Practical details

Antares Field Guide Training Centre (antares.co.za) runs 88-day courses in Balule North Nature Reserve, and has a good record of placing graduates at game lodges around South Africa. See the website of the **Field Guide Association of South Africa** (fgasa.co.za) for other operators. Peak season for wildlife viewing is June to September.

Other options

Choose your favourite animal and get tracking – locate turtles and mighty marine mammals in the bathtub-warm waters around Mauritius, go bush and take tips from Aboriginal trackers on a bushcraft course in outback Australia or seek everything from wolves to cougars on a wildlife-tracking course in the American northwest through the **Wilderness Awareness School** (wildernessawareness.org).

Doing it at home

Opportunities to track prides of lions are probably pretty thin on the ground back home, but why not get close to the local wildlife? The skills you use to track wildebeest can easily be modified to tracking whatever runs wild where you live.

WHAT TO EXPECT

Adventurers wanted! Watching wildlife from the back of a jeep is nothing compared to the giddy thrill of tracking your own lion across the savannah.

Picture the scene: the ranger stops suddenly and raises a hand, stooping to examine a set of dusty tracks within the parched grasses. He listens intently, sniffs the air. 'Lions,' he says. 'They're close.'

Well, that could be you. Joining a

Track big game across the veldt then sleep out beneath African skies – it's all part of the package on a game-ranger course in South Africa.

game-ranger course means digging deep into your pockets, but can you really put a price on the exhilaration of getting this close to the world's top predators, in their own natural surroundings?

Hobby courses abound, but for the real deal, sign up for Level I Nature Guide or Level I Tracker Guide. Veteran rangers will teach you how to locate big beasties – and stay safe

while you do it – at nature reserves teeming with Africa's signature species: lions, rhinos, cheetahs, elephants and hyenas. Immersed in the same environment as the wildlife, you'll learn the hands-on skills of tracking, sorting predators from prey, identifying tracks and even recognising animals by their spoor.

So pick your specialism – birds, herding mammals, snakes and

reptiles or big predators – and you'll get a chance for your own close encounter. In the process you'll acquire essential skills like firearms handling, off-road 4WD driving, and knowing when to back off as well as move in. Pass the final examination and you can seek work as a game ranger – just in case you don't fancy going back to the office after the thrill of tracking leopards.

As a rookie field guide you will experience wildlife in its most spectacular state.

EAT LIKE A LOCAL TO BECOME A NEW YORKER

Duration Two to four hours ✳ **Cost** US$50 to $150 ✳ **Outcome** A full belly, and a new appreciation for New York's history and the term 'culinary melting pot' ✳ **Where** New York City, US

How it suits you

Don't just see New York; *be* New York. And the best way to live like a local is to munch your way to the heart of this food-obsessed metropolis on a guided tour. Intrepid travellers will love slipping behind the tourist veneer of the big city by visiting neighbourhood eateries (especially if you take a tour in one of the lesser-touristed outer boroughs). If you're into history, these tours are edible education, covering broad themes (centuries of migration) and intensely local lore and legend.

What you'll get from it

★ **Street sense** Those unprepossessing shop fronts you've been walking past without taking a second glance are actually relics of food history; after your tour, you'll know what to look for.
★ **Insight** Exploring a neighbourhood with an expert will help you feel the undercurrents of history and open up the city.
★ **Food icons** Tick off some of those once-in-a-lifetime food experiences – a real New York frankfurter (ideally from Nathan's Famous in Coney Island), a Reuben sandwich, a whitefish bagel, an egg cream.

Practical details

Try **Foods of New York** (foodsofny.com) for walking tours in Manhattan, or **Famous Fat Dave's Five Borough Eating Tour on the Wheels of Steel** (famousfatdave.com) – no further explanation required. Walking tours will require sturdy footwear; whether you're on foot or wheels, you'll need a good appetite and a ready-for-anything palate.

Other options

You'll find food tours with a multicultural bent in most major cities – try Indian food walks in London; explorations of San Francisco's little Italy; or walking 'safaris' of Sydney's Greek, Turkish and Lebanese suburbs.

Doing it at home

If you live in a city where immigration has influenced the local food scene, see if you can track down a home-town food tour. And if not, do your own – visit a neighbourhood you don't usually get to and explore the variety of exotic eateries you might find there. How do they reflect the history and ethnic breakdown of your town? Don't forget, sampling is compulsory!

WHAT TO EXPECT

New York is a city created by immigrants. As each wave – Germans, Italians, European Jews, Mexicans, West Africans among countless others – arrived, settled and dispersed throughout the country, they left an edible legacy, an archaeological dig of cuisines that's part of the joy of visiting the city.

New York food tours are usually on foot, the street-pounding regularly

Graduate as an honorary New Yorker by taking a bite of the Big Apple. A fieldtrip of the city's food scene teaches you everything about eating like a local.

interrupted by pausing to sample the neighbourhood's goodies. You might wander around SoHo, a century-old Italian neighbourhood, dropping into a classic red-sauce joint established in 1918 and tasting the handmade mozzarella at Joe's Dairy. In the Lower East Side you might visit Russ & Daughters, a mainstay of the Jewish community since 1914, serving specialities like bagels with cream cheese and more varieties of smoked salmon than you thought possible. A local Cuban place in the Village, the best Hong Kong–style dumplings in Chinatown – all are served up with a side of neighbourhood gossip and local lore by your guide, often a long-term local resident.

Not all tours focus on Manhattan – you can tour Brooklyn while eating pizza (which locals maintain is better than anything you'll get across the East River) or take a checker-cab tour of the Bronx for Jamaican jerk shrimp and West African soul food. Wherever you go, you're guaranteed an insight into New York, how it came to be, how it all still fits together so well, and why the city that never sleeps spends plenty of its waking hours eating.

Tasty tours run by local foodies reveal NYC's hottest eateries.

SOAR LIKE AN EAGLE
OVER THE HIMALAYAS

Duration From one hour to five or more days ✳ **Cost** From £115 ✳ **Outcome** Exhilaration, off-the-scale adrenalin and the chance to glide like a hawk ✳ **Where** Pokhara, Nepal

Use thermal updrafts to gain a bird's-eye view of Nepal.

Let trained birds of prey guide you through the thermals spiralling up from Nepal's mist-shrouded valleys; now that's what 'free as a bird' really means.

WHAT TO EXPECT

In the foothills of the Himalaya, birds of prey spiral overhead like leaves in the breeze. Inspired by their flight, British thrill-seeker Scott Mason set up camp in Pokhara and came up with the radical idea of combining the twin disciplines of paragliding and falconry. The goal? To tap into the innate ability of these avian predators to locate thermal updrafts and prolong unpowered flight. And so the eccentric sport of parahawking was born.

Today, Pokhara is the undisputed capital of parahawking. On tandem flights, trained vultures tag along for the ride like feathered spirit guides, steering you towards soaring updrafts that sweep over the mountain valleys. Even better, you don't need years of training to participate, and between flights you can hang with hawkers, fraternise with the bird life or set off to explore the foothills of the Annapurna range at ground level, rambling through hill villages and terraced padi fields.

Should you feel the urge to take things further, Pokhara's parahawkers offer falconry lessons that will get you under the skin (or feathers) of these magnificent birds. Combine that with solo paragliding training and you'll experience the closest thing to flying like a bird since Icarus got too close to the sun.

It takes time and dedication to train up to Solo Pilot, and even longer to train a bird of prey. If a tandem flight gives you the buzz, talk to Scott about the next steps towards becoming a birdman of the Himalayas. Parahawking is not just a hobby – it's a way of life. A particularly laid-back way of life.

How it suits you

If Lynyrd Skynyrd's 'Free Bird' is the unofficial soundtrack to your life, parahawking is probably for you. Learning to fly like an eagle is a pursuit for intrepid explorers and can-do adventurers, though anyone with a spontaneous edge will appreciate the freedom of a laid-back lifestyle on the shores of Pokhara's Phewa Lake. And a little engineering know-how won't hold you back if you decide to make parahawking a vocation.

What you'll get from it

★ **Adrenalin** Feel your pulse racing as the ground drops away beneath your feet and you launch into the ether ...
★ **Serenity** Parahawking is not a high-five, hell-yeah kind of sport; tracking a trained hawk across the sky is closer to *Kes* than *Point Break*.
★ **Brownie points** Every flight includes a donation to fund bird conservation in the Himalaya.
★ **A sense of wonder** Who could fail to be moved by the experience of seeing the Himalaya through an eagle's eyes?

Practical details

Tandem **parahawking** (parahawking.com) flights and falconry courses run from the Maya Devi Resort near Pokhara from November to March.

Other options

Want more wildlife interaction? Take swimming lessons from dolphins at **Akaroa** (swimmingwithdolphins.co.nz) in New Zealand, seek inspiration from monkeys on a climbing course in Koh Phi Phi, Thailand, or let camels show you the right way to do deserts, on a safari in the Sahara.

Doing it at home

The primary obstacles to parahawking at home are a lack of birds of prey and mountains. But should you be lucky enough to live close to the hilly wilds, consider training up as a solo paraglider and joining your local falconry club.

MAKE A SONG AND DANCE ABOUT BEIJING OPERA

Duration One day ✴ **Cost** 150 yuan ✴ **Outcome** You'll get a taste of it all – singing, dancing, acrobatics and sword fighting – while dressed in flowing silk ✴ **Where** Beijing, China

Journey to the home of a centuries-old form of drama that combines multiple talents and shines the spotlight on Chinese culture.

WHAT TO EXPECT

Beijing (or Peking) opera is more pantomime than Western opera. Listen to those clashing cymbals ushering in the soldiers in draped golden silk. The movements are exaggerated and erratic. The actors speak in high jagged voices and then cartwheel, fluttering their headpieces like flags, captivating you enough to want to try it yourself.

You put on the masklike makeup, rendering your face reminiscent of a yin-yang symbol. The choice is a white-faced style to reflect a vicious soul, or black for a selfless hero. While you consult your conscience, your robe is layered on – swish your arms and its 'water sleeves' flap with purple embroidery, announcing that you are a high-ranking official in ancient China, naturally. In this outfit, you'll try your first beautiful leap.

Yes, every movement must be beautiful: that is the key. Stand tall in the 'mountain' pose, and move fluidly to perform the 'cloud', which feels part tai chi, part dance.

Now it's time to say something – and sing, because speaking in Beijing opera has musicality. And don't expect the high-pitched *jinghu* (two-stringed instrument) to cushion your voice – it zigzags at a different speed and pitch around you.

And every movement represents something. A tug in the air means getting on a horse, and one revolution on the stage is all it takes to travel across a whole desert. You'll get it, don't cry – just dab at your cheek symbolically.

How it suits you

Time-travelling history buffs will find that all of China's literature, history, mythology and culture are instilled in Beijing opera's movements, words, makeup and costume. For the people person, being on stage and being allowed to be dramatic was written in your stars. And for the artistic traveller, the detailed costumes and highly symbolic makeup will inspire your own creations.

What you'll get from it

★ **Confidence** Being dressed head to toe as a Beijing opera character is great training for expressing yourself when you simply dressed in jeans and a T-shirt.
★ **Insight into people** Acting out the basic young/old, rich/poor, wise/clown characters makes you appreciate the unique mix of types that go into every personality around you.
★ **Discipline** You can get a taster of Beijing opera but it takes dedication and years of hard work to become a professional. Traditionally, the pros started as children.

Practical details

China Culture Center (chinaculturecenter.org) in Beijing is a workshop run by two professional actors, who explain and perform the movements, makeup and dress. Time is provided for you to try on costumes and participate. Also in Beijing, the **International Centre for Beijing Opera** (beijingopera. info) conducts an introductory 'Beijing opera demystified' course, which includes hands-on workshops. Tailored short and longer courses that run for years are also available, and all classes are conducted in English and Chinese languages.

Other options

In the UK, the **London Jing Kun Opera Association** (londonjingkunopera.co.uk) conducts workshops on Beijing opera's music, face painting and performance.

Doing it at home

Now that you know how to perform Chinese-style, how will you bring the drama home? Join a local theatre group? Stage your own Beijing opera or offer face-painting classes to children? Navigate the rising and falling terrain of the tonal Chinese language?

A lick of paint will transform you into an operatic character.

MAKE (AND EAT) FINE CHOCOLATE IN PARIS

Duration Half a day ✳ **Cost** €250 ✳ **Outcome** Your next party trick will really dazzle your mates – who doesn't like chocolate for dessert? ✳ **Where** The Ritz, Paris, France

How it suits you

For the culinary traveller, this is a no brainer. Cooking courses *in situ* are one of the best ways to get to know a destination's culture and culinary techniques. For the social butterfly, they're a great way to meet fellow travellers. There's a certain sense of bonding (you'll often be sampling what others have made) and shared achievement at the completion of a course. Of course, don't forget to celebrate your new-found friendships at a local bistro!

What you'll get from it

★ **Method** While you can learn to make chocolate desserts from cookbooks, TV shows or YouTube videos, there's really no substitute for real-life experience – especially one led by top chefs speaking in French-inflected English.
★ **Culture** The French are renowned for their world-class food. Case in point: Frenchman André Jules Michelin started the famed Michelin guide. Get under the skin of the French school of cooking by taking this class.
★ **Bragging rights** Imagine the accolades you'll get next time you take a tray of 'chocolate and Périgord black truffle macaroons' to a dinner party. Ooh la la!

Practical details

Classes at **École Ritz Escoffier** (www.ritzescoffier.com) start at three hours and stretch out to a 19-week course. Short courses are held most weekends.

Other options

For chocolate cookery options outside Paris, try the **Savour Chocolate & Patisserie School** (savourschool.com.au) in Melbourne, Manchester's **Slattery Patissier & Chocolatier** (slattery.co.uk) or Chicago's **Chocolate Academy** (chocolate-academy.com).

Doing it at home

Start by practising – there's no better way to remember the skills you've learnt than by re-creating your culinary masterpieces at home and for dinner parties. Better yet, get friends and family members to sample your yummy treats (Christmas presents sorted!) and you'll probably get inundated with requests for lessons.

WHAT TO EXPECT

Extreme chocolate alert! Paris has cooking schools galore but a chocolate-making class at the École Ritz Escoffier school takes you one step closer to culinary perfection.

As the father of modern French cooking, Auguste Escoffier, famously said, 'Good cooking is the foundation of true happiness.' How true. He was also

Ah, Paris, the city of love. And what better aphrodisiac than chocolate? Why not combine the two, and master the art of making chocolate in the world's most romantic city?

the first executive chef at the glitzy hotel Ritz, where the École Ritz Escoffier has teamed up with La Maison du Chocolat to host this Extreme Chocolate class.

The three-hour workshop will equip you with all the skills to make *haute cuisine* chocolate desserts such as 'cubist mi-cuit foie gras, dark chocolate and Sanshou pepper, dipped in a pink Champagne frappe', 'chocolate and Périgord black truffle macaroons' and 'thyme-infused ice cream, crushed Swiss rocher, and hot chocolate soup'.

Learning to mix, melt, stir and fold, you'll be handling top-quality ingredients in a well-equipped environment, taking instructions from some of the best chefs in the business.

Of course, if you're really, really, *really* crazy about chocolate, you can opt to attend a six-day course (from €3200) at Ecole du Grand Chocolat school run by the famed Valrhona chocolate company in their HQ at Tain L'Hermitage, a small town four hours from Paris.

At the course's end, sample your yummy handiwork.

HUNT AND GATHER IN NAMIBIA

Duration From three days ✳ **Cost** From N$1200 per day ✳ **Outcome** A greater understanding of a unique culture, and a meaner shot with a bow ✳ **Where** Bushmanland, northeast Namibia

Live out in the desert with one of last San communities – track porcupines and drink honey from the hive.

WHAT TO EXPECT

The Bushmen are not born teachers. Sign up for a 'course' here and you won't be summoned to a dusty classroom for lessons. No, a stay with the San is more watch-and-see: you simply spectate as they get on with their fast-vanishing way of life.

Each morning there's a confab: men and women discussing the needs of the day – more mangeti nuts, perhaps some honey, or a nice big porcupine for supper. Just your run-of-the-mill shopping list in northeast Namibia.

Decision made (usually by the ladies), the loin-clothed hunters are despatched with their bows – and you go along for the ride. The outing could last a few hours, maybe all day: the idea is not to return to camp empty-handed.

It can be exhausting keeping up with these wiry pros, supremely adept at negotiating the baking-hot scrub and not impaling their tender parts on acacia thorns along the way. The San will stop, now and then, to point out features (via your translator): the leaves that double as medicine, the aardvark burrows and termite mounds, the fresh tracks of a prowling leopard …

Come evening, while (with luck) the porcupine's roasting on the fire, and songs and game-playing giggles fill the air. And as the final embers snuff out to leave the celestial sparkle utterly undiluted, you'll start to wonder what else – besides the smiles of friends and the next day's meal – you really need.

How it suits you

You need to be both an adventurer and a social butterfly to get the most from this experience. Tracking with the Bushmen can be physically demanding, but more important is your attitude: these are sociable, uninhibited people who do not understand reticence or introversion. Join in with every monkey orange game – regardless of whether you get the rules. Sing along to the tunes with gusto – even though you might sound like an injured hyena.

What you'll get from it

★ **Life skills** You never know when you might need to make a fire without using a match.
★ **Perspective** Watching people survive with only the possessions they can fit in an animal-skin satchel might make you think twice about buying that iPad.
★ **Bush-savvy** Learn to read the wilderness like the Bushmen do: the paw prints, the shadows, the birds – all contain info that could end up saving your life.
★ **Serenity** Let the smell of the campfire and the twinkle of stars provide a slow-down from the modern world.

Practical details

Nhoma Safari Camp (www.tsumkwel.iway.na), 80km from Tsumkwe, is wholly owned by the Ju'hoansi San community. It has 10 rustic rooms, plus space for a few tents.

Other options

Stay at **Edo's Camp** (edoscamp.com) in Botswana's Central Kalahari, to visit the neighbouring Bushman Village. Venture into Arnhem Land (see p116-117), a remote slice of Australia's Northern Territory, to learn the traditional skills of the local Aborigines, or step out with the Huaorani of Ecuador's Oriente to see how this tribe survives amid the Amazon.

Doing it at home

While it's unlikely (and not encouraged) that you'll start hunting squirrels in the park or ditching your trousers for a loincloth, the simplicity of Bushman lifestyle is something you can transfer to your daily grind. For a start, you could try discarding some of those bleeping, flashing distractions for an earthier existence based on community.

Bushmen look for lunch
in northeast Namibia.

JOIN A TREEVOLUTION IN CAPE TOWN

Duration One day ✳ **Cost** 450 rand ✳ **Outcome** Gardening savvy, grubby fingers and a fuzzy warm feeling inside ✳ **Where** Cape Town, South Africa

How it suits you

Planting trees is sweaty and dirty work, but it's also immediately rewarding. Start-up social enterprise Greenpop also needs people for back-office and organisational jobs, and internees with skills from computing to marketing. This is the project for an altruistic type who wants to connect meaningfully with all manner of Southern Africans, while learning something of their cultures and daily living challenges.

What you'll get from it

★ **Green fingers** Learn gardening techniques that will help your saplings flourish into mighty boughs, and recycling tips such as using grey water from your bath to water the plants.
★ **Horticultural know-how** Discover why Brazilian pepper trees, Australian eucalyptus and English oaks are not assisting Southern African biodiversity.
★ **Team management** On planting days at schools you can help the child volunteers fulfil their allotted team roles, including quality controller, beautifier or member of the fun police.

Practical details

Tree-planting programs in Cape Town are run by **Greenpop** (greenpop.org). Every Wednesday is usually a volunteer tree-tour day. Greenpop also runs an ongoing project to plant trees in Livingstone, Zambia, that needs volunteers and interns.

Other options

There are several Latin American tree-planting options, including Nicaragua's **Las Mercedes Reforestation Project** (nicaraguareforestationproject.org), Costa Rica's **Cloudbridge Nature Reserve** (cloudbridge.org) project and Ecuador's **Cloud Forest Reserve** (ecovolunteerup.org) reforestation project, where you can help provide a refuge for endangered Andean bears. You can learn about creating inner-city green spaces in Australia at Melbourne's **Urban Reforestation** (urbanreforestation.com), or check out the **Alamanga Reforestation** (tree-nation.com) project in Madagascar.

Doing it at home

If you don't have your own backyard in which to plant a tree or other greenery, hook up with local reforestation programs or check with your local authority about getting an allotment.

WHAT TO EXPECT

Make like a tree and leave – for Cape Town, where the Greenpop organisation is spreading a carpet of green around the city.

Greenpop has planted close on 10,000 trees in schools, communities and deforested areas in Cape Town, across the Western Cape of South Africa and further afield. Roll up your sleeves and

Reforestation is not only fun but also educational when you plant a tree in Cape Town – branch out for a hands-on lesson in horticulture and harvest insights into day-to-day life in South Africa.

join in major events like the Heritage Day of a Thousand Trees, which saw 1000 trees planted in Mannenberg, one of Cape Town's most deprived and crime-ridden areas.

Greenpop regularly runs planting days, so join in to learn some garden know-how from experts with green thumbs. You'll find out how deep you should bury your tree, and how to mix the soil with fertiliser. Take home tips on how to get rid of grasses and weeds from the surrounding soil, how to turn your plant so it faces the nurturing rays of the sun, and how to water your tree so it keeps on growing.

The United Nations estimates that the world's forest area has decreased by 30 million hectares since 1990 – an area larger than Argentina. The solution – to plant more trees – is simple, and you may already be doing this indirectly by contributing to carbon-offsetting schemes. With Greenpop, you can learn how to plant your own tree and care for it so it reaches maturity, while helping to create beauty out of a wasteland.

Cape Town is the setting for Greenpop's fresh thinking.

PAINT EASTER EGGS IN UKRAINE

Duration Two days ✳ **Cost** From €160 ✳ **Outcome** A beautiful hand-decorated ornament and an appreciation for chocolate-free Easter eggs ✳ **Where** Kosmach, Ukraine

Learn the hidden meaning behind designs and the skills of using wax and handmade dyes in the Ukrainian tradition of Easter-egg painting.

WHAT TO EXPECT

Painting Easter eggs is a big deal in Eastern Europe, but only in Ukraine will you see age-old batik-style wax and hand-applied-colour techniques in action. The intricate traditional designs still carry deep meanings here, and to knowledgeable Ukrainians the provenance of the painted eggs, called *pysanky,* is instantly revealed by their unique motifs.

The Hutsuls – an ethno-cultural group of Ukrainian highlanders who have preserved their traditional way of life in the Carpathian Mountains – are known for their *pysanky*-producing skills. Indeed, an ancient belief is that if they abandoned this art there could be a spread of terrible evil throughout the world.

Egg painting has always been a frenzied activity a month before Easter, but many crafts-minded Hutsul villagers now engage in the pastime year-round. So any time of year, get yourself to the remote Carpathian community of Kosmach to learn the art from a *pysanky* master in the heart of Hutsul heritage.

By watching and practising, you'll learn about the different designs and their long history, then have a go at replicating the *pysanky* master's meticulous painting techniques. What might once have seemed like unassuming decoration is revealed to be replete with talismanic or religious importance, each line and dot invested with significance.

How it suits you

Anyone with an artistic temperament and a great attention to detail is particularly well adapted to painting *pysanky*. As with many crafts, coming to grips with the tools and techniques is half the challenge, as drawing with a wax-tipped stylus is not as easy as it sounds. Planning what to etch before each dip into a different dye (progressing from lightest to darkest colour) takes careful forethought, so the more patient and pedantic you are, the better the result.

What you'll get from it

★ **Cultural insight** Painting *pysanky* exposes you to a special side of Ukraine that few tourists observe. A day with the Hutsuls puts you in touch with a unique traditional society.
★ **Community connection** Your master class is held in the home of a local artisan, providing insights into the lifestyle of rural people in Ukraine.
★ **Warm glow** Class fees go a long way, contributing to the local community by helping to preserve family heritage and ancient customs.

Practical details

The Kosmach private master class is part of a two-day Hutsul experience that also includes a day spent engaged in your host family's typical daily activities and a visit to Hutsul highland shepherds. Find more details at **Gunyah** (www.gunyah.com, click on Ukraine).

Other options

There is no shortage of opportunities to decorate an egg, especially in the *pysanky* style and particularly around Easter, with a practised professional to help you master the tools. To find a wide range of patterns online, search for 'egg decorating ethnic patterns' on the web and marvel at the results.

Doing it at home

The essential tools of *pysanky* painting – wax, stylus and dye – are widely available, as are many traditional patterns from Ukraine and elsewhere. Newly empowered by a master practitioner and armed with a few tricks of the trade, you can use your egg-design acumen to impress all comers.

Painted decorations are thought
to ward off evil spirits.

Music & Dance

BE SWEPT OFF YOUR FEET IN BARCELONA

Duration One hour to five days ✱ **Cost** From €3 a lesson ✱ **Outcome** Rhythm (hopefully) – the aim is to move your feet and swish your hips with style and abandon ✱ **Where** Barcelona, Spain

Make friends and burn calories with every salsa step.

Come dancing in Barcelona – spend your days learning salsa steps in sweaty studios and your nights in the city's legendary clubs, busting your new moves.

WHAT TO EXPECT

Expect sore toes, tangled arms, sweat and embarrassment. Expect to get uncomfortably close to short men named Luis (or lovelies named Lucia). Expect to try, fail and try again. Then maybe – just maybe – expect it all to start making sense ...

Learning salsa in Barcelona is not entirely authentic. The dance form originated in 1920s Cuba, where the music traditions of European *danzón*, African *yambú*, Caribbean *son* and more melded into this spicy hip-shaker.

But the Catalans have adopted the genre with gusto – it seems to suit their flamboyant nature, their beach-side sun-soaked environs and their general lust for life. As such, Barcelona is writhing with sultry *salsarinas*, clubs a-thump with eight-beat rhythms and – mercifully – studios where you can learn the steps.

It's not a difficult dance to pick up – anyone can master the basic 'mambo' step; most, with tuition, can add a few flourishes (perhaps a side-to-side shimmy or underarm twizzle). Getting good is another matter entirely, but a few hours with an expert will see you able to brave the city's dance floors, if not quite set them on fire.

A lot depends on your partner, too – salsa is a dance of instinct and synergy. But the main thing is to give it a go: take a final slurp of emboldening mojito and hit the floor with dash and daring. After all, it's better to fail spectacularly than not to try at all.

How it suits you

This is an escapade for social butterflies – those comfortable with rubbing up next to strangers of the opposite sex, in rooms full of people doing likewise. This is also a dance for the spontaneous traveller: there are set moves in salsa, of course, but much of the skill is about feeling the music and the rhythm of your partner – and responding accordingly. Memorising routines and step-counting in your head is not embracing the Latino spirit.

What you'll get from it

★ **Rhythm** With luck, you'll develop more swing to your step, more swish in your hips, more sauce to your salsa.

★ **Grace** It's not just about learning the technicalities: you'll gain poise and style, too. Or at least manage to wobble over less often.

★ **Confidence** Weed out your inner wallflower – a few Spanish salsa lessons will make you bolder, both in terms of practising the moves and the local lingo.

★ **Fitness** Count on burning around 300 calories an hour, upping your aerobic capacity and trimming down those thighs.

Practical details

Several companies offer salsa lessons in Barcelona. **Club Dance Holidays** (clubdanceholidays.co.uk) can arrange weekend breaks, while **Go Learn To** (golearnto.com) combines salsa and Spanish-language courses. **Antilla BCN Latin Club** (antillasalsa.com), Barcelona's biggest salsa venue, also runs a dance school.

Other options

Take up tango in Buenos Aires (see p210-211) – oh-so-patient teachers abound in the Argentine capital; try the districts of La Boca and San Telmo. Find a frilly skirt for flamenco fun in Seville, Granada or Jerez in Andalusia (see p144-145). Or pay a visit to **Blackpool** (www.blackpooldancefestival.com) in northwest England, strictly the home of ballroom, to waltz and quick-step across the town's hallowed dance floor.

Doing it at home

Dancing is the new black; it's so hot right now, you'll want to salsa everywhere – from nightclubs to bus stops. It's a fabulous way to make new friends.

Art & Crafts

GET CARRIED AWAY
DRAWING MANGA

Duration Two weeks ❋ **Cost** ¥79,000 ❋ **Outcome** An ability to express emotions with just the eyes, maintain permanently windswept hair, and spell Japanese sound effects ❋ **Where** Fukuoka, Japan

How it suits you

Artistic travellers will get to express their inner world on paper, and not just in dramatic crash-boom ways. The repetition and discipline involved in drawing manga will appeal to meditative minds and orderly types who'll love the precision involved in making every line just right. And hermits will find it's easier to draw people than having to deal with them.

What you'll get from it

★ **Daydreaming** Silent concentration with your mind's eye leads to wondering what your inner hero will do next.
★ **Precision** One dash around the eyes can turn disappointment into excitement.
★ **An ear for details** Thinking about how you spell anger or sorrow makes you notice the world of sound around you. In a language made up of short syllables, such as Japanese, tiny utterances are important.
★ **Laughter** You realise how ridiculous real life is when you capture it on paper with exaggerated muscles, eyes and hair.

Practical details

The **WAHAHA Japanese Language School** (wahahanihongo.com) in Fukuoka offers manga classes that include additional Japanese lessons, spread over two weeks.

Other options

The **Japanese Study School** (japanesestudyschool.com) organises manga classes in central London, as well as home tutoring. In Australia, **OzTAKU** (oztaku.com) runs a range of manga classes in libraries for both children and adults.

Doing it at home

Now that you've drawn the first page of your manga series, how will you bring the drama to your own life? Set up shop at a market drawing people? Learn Japanese? Manga in Japan extends to fashion and music, so you could get serious about it and incorporate it into your everyday style or in a costume at a manga convention.

WHAT TO EXPECT

Wooow! says your speech bubble. Is that a famous manga artist you see before you?

Modern manga can be subtle, filmic even. It's read by women and people of all ages, and is often respected as legitimate art.

At manga school, you'll learn to capture a story as a one-page Japanese-style comic, but first your instructor wants to know who is bursting to get out of you

Go all dewy-eyed in the birthplace of Akira and Astro Boy, sketching your own comic book complete with dragon hair – and sound effects you can see.

and onto the sketchpad. An eco superwarrior? A bionic schoolgirl?

You'll learn how to draw your characters using professional tools: special pens to produce thick or thin lines with the inks; tracing paper to get that spiky hair just right; cutters and rulers to shift elements into the right place. And adding backgrounds is easier with the equipment too – trees slanting away, or something more unusual such as a storm of computer parts.

Ahem, roll sound, please. You'll learn that manga sound effects are visual – rising like skyscrapers or almost vanishing in dotted lines. So whether the noise of your salaryman character's heart breaking is 'tek', 'pwop!' or 'waaAAH!!', you'll learn how to put these sounds into words.

The shape of the letters form part of the art, but why stop with English? Manga classes are backed up with Japanese-language lessons too. You'll study manga the way it was meant to be read – in Japanese – so you can learn to draw kanji script floating above your hero's head. It also looks way cool.

Eye for opportunity: manga is a $3bn business in Japan.

MORPH INTO A MUAY THAI WARRIOR

Duration From a single session to a month ✳ **Cost** From US$30 ✳ **Outcome** The ultimate work-out, buff pecs and a deeper understanding of Thailand's national sport ✳ **Where** Pattaya, Thailand

Join a training camp in Thailand to learn the secrets of a lethal traditional martial art from seasoned fighters.

WHAT TO EXPECT

Punch, kick and elbow your way through a Muay Thai training session and you'll gain a keen appreciation of just how dedicated fighters need to be to reach the top. Your trainer could well have begun fighting as a mere lad, and spent decades perfecting his art.

Typically, sessions start with a 6km warm-up run along the beach (cue 'Eye of the Tiger') or furiously jumping rope. Thai fighters with hundreds of fights under their belt then guide you through five rounds of one-on-one pad work, offering advice on technique.

You'll learn how to strike using all eight points of contact (two hands, elbows, knees and feet) and how to block using your knees. With two sessions each day, you'll also practise bag work and some sparring and clinching, crucial elements of this particular martial art. It's not all testosterone-fuelled carnage though – working with the Thai trainers is a fun and relaxed experience as these guys have nothing left to prove to anyone.

Muay Thai has a rich history and those wanting to know more can also learn how to perform the ritualistic dance known as *wai kru ram muay*, performed by fighters before every fight to ask the spirits for protection and to pay respects to their trainer.

How it suits you

For those who want to gain a better understanding of Thai culture and mix with locals, Muay Thai ticks both boxes. A large part of training involves self-discipline and respect, both important tenets of Buddhism. Looking for some action? Nothing pumps the adrenalin harder than the feel of fists and feet smacking leather pads. Age and gender are no barrier: anyone from eight to 80 can take part and, increasingly, more health-conscious women are pulling on their gloves.

What you'll get from it

★ **Fitness** When it comes to work-outs and fitness regimes, few routines burn calories like this.
★ **Satisfaction** A post-session pat on the back is required, if your aching muscles can still stretch that far.
★ **Understanding** Discover the rituals associated with Muay Thai, from the hypnotic music to the special headgear *(mongkol)* and armbands *(pra jiad)*.

Practical details

From novice to professional pugilist, anyone can train. Some walk-in visitors just want a single sessions while others sign up for a month or more. Fully inclusive on-site accommodation and airport pick-ups are available. Visit **Fairtex Muay Thai Pattaya** (fairtex-muaythai.com) for details.

Other options

The fascination with Muay Thai is now international, with training camps and fighting arenas in many countries. In the US, check out the California-based **Muay Thai School USA** (muaythaischoolusa.com). To find a club in the UK, visit **Muay Thai Clubs UK** (muaythaiclubs.co.uk), while for those in Australia there's the **Bulldog Gym** (bulldoggym. com.au) in Sydney.

Doing it at home

Once you've mastered the basics, it's simple to continue your new fitness regime anywhere. Muay Thai's growing popularity means there could well be a gym in your neighbourhood. If you are serious about Muay Thai, you could even find out where fights are held and put your new skills to the test.

Muay thai gyms are spartan
but welcome newcomers.

EMBRACE THE VOODOO
SPIRIT IN GHANA

Duration Six hours ✷ **Cost** US$39 ✷ **Outcome** Insights into West Africa's religious heritage, health tips from a voodoo priest and some new dance moves ✷ **Where** Kumasi, Ghana

Discover the voodoo chile within on a hands-on visit to a genuine Ghanaian voodoo priest.

WHAT TO EXPECT

Want to learn how herbs and roots are used throughout Ghana for curing ailments, then throw your body into a voodoo dance? Read on ...

Practised in West Africa for centuries, voodoo is more than a belief system. It is a complete way of life, anchored in culture, philosophy, dance, music and ritual. The forces of nature are also an integral part of the faith: trees, rocks, plants and rivers are all important elements of voodoo, believed to be spirit habitats and sources of divinely inspired power.

All this and more is explained to you and put in its proper context, before you are introduced to one of Kumasi's voodoo priests. First, an experienced local guide takes you on an afternoon stroll to explore local markets and bodies of water, clarifying their connections to the priest.

Then, at an appointed evening hour, you get to share time with the priest in his sacred location near the source of his power, essential to its potency. The priest explains the power of roots, herbs and dance to ease illness the traditional way and demonstrates their uses. If you're into it, a private consultation might follow.

In return for the priest's services – and perhaps a small supply of tonics, creams or tinctures – a bottle of schnapps is offered, often poured onto the shrine to summon spirits.

How it suits you

Given voodoo's history as a traditional and faith-based form of holistic and homeopathic healing, if you're a spiritual type you may find a private consultation with the priest brings profound solace. Those with an academic curiosity about how voodoo is practised will also be intrigued by this experience.

What you'll get from it

★ **Cultural insight** You come away with a solid understanding of the history and practices of the Ashanti people.
★ **Spiritual healing** Traditional beliefs hold that a private consultation may result in relief from everything from fevers and migraines to burns and more serious diseases, not to mention improvements in emotional fortune.
★ **Knowledge of natural medicine** Seeing the use of herbs and roots leads to an understanding of alternative remedies for stomach ulcers, headaches, body pain and more.

Practical details

Urban Adventures (urbanadventures.com, click on Ghana) can arrange your voodoo voyage throughout the year. Keep in mind that locals get their voodoo dose in greater numbers at the beginning and end of each year, and during the Akwasidae festival.

Other options

West Africa's voodoo trail leads to Togo, Benin and Burkina Faso – look for tours that take you there. For New Orleans voodoo workshops, try **Bloody Mary's Tours** (bloodymarystours.com). Or explore other spiritual practices, maybe ayurveda, freemasonry, Hermetic Qabalah, hoodoo, Tameran Wicca or Rastafarianism.

Doing it at home

While unsupervised experimentation with naturally occurring medicinal products is not encouraged, your new elementary knowledge of alternative sources of healing could, with guidance, help you find nonallopathic ways to improve your mind and body health. Of course, the voodoo dance moves you learn could also kick-start a spiritually uplifting healing process.

The voodoo you do has its roots in West African tradition.

SORT THE REAL MEN
FROM THE SNOWMEN

Duration From six days ✳ **Cost** Courses from C$990 per day ✳ **Outcome** A sense of self-reliance and Arctic survival skills ✳ **Where** Nunavik, northern Quebec, Canada

How it suits you

Adventure comes with the territory in the Arctic. On day one, you won't want to come out of your sleeping bag; by the time you finish, you'll be half human, half polar bear. In fact, polar bears are one of many hazards you might encounter on your travels. This is definitely a course for do-ers – practical people who enjoy a challenge and don't mind strenuous effort, fatigue and extreme cold.

What you'll get from it

★ **Native wisdom** Without the survival know-how of indigenous peoples, great explorers like Peary and Shackleton wouldn't have lasted a day.
★ **Skills** Who wouldn't want to be able to navigate by the stars, light a fire in the wild or survive a night in the open?
★ **Exhilaration** Challenging nature and coming out on top is always a rush; that goes double with frostbite nipping at your heels.
★ **Satisfaction** Venturing into the wild is one thing – it's coming out again alive that brings the sense of accomplishment!

Practical details

Winter survival courses at the **Nunavik Arctic Survival Training Center** (nastc.ca) run from January to April. The only way to reach Nunavik is by air, with flights from Montreal.

Other options

Several operators offer week-long courses in the far north of Sweden from US$1900. Seek survival skills from the Sami on a training course in Laponia, northern Sweden, with **Wildwood Bushcraft** (wildwoodbushcraft.com), or prepare yourself for the push to the Pole with polar travel training in Greenland through **Pirhuk** (expeditiongreenland.com). If you can get permission, or happen to be a research scientist, join a snowcraft course in Antarctica. To fine-tune your igloo-building skills see p204-205.

Doing it at home

How much you get to use your winter skills will depend on the climate back home. But when you plan your next holiday, pick up brochures for Svalbard, Greenland and Antarctica.

WHAT TO EXPECT

Before we say anything else, be ready for some serious cold. In the Arctic, night-time temperatures can plummet to -50°C, colder than an industrial deep-freeze. In this remote landscape, snow-blindness, hypothermia, dehydration and frostbite are ever-present dangers. If you don't want to end up next to the frozen peas, you'll need to pay close attention.

Find your inner Inuit – or rather dig them out of the snow – on an Arctic survival course with native teachers in the windswept wilderness of northern Canada.

So why put yourself in this perilous predicament? Well, for one thing, you'll get to plug into the wisdom of people who have been surviving in this inhospitable environment for thousands of years. Courses at the Nunavik Arctic Survival Training Center are run by Inuit teachers with the tundra in their blood. Expensive thermal gear is no substitute for

learning how to navigate, forage and thrive in the frozen wastes from the descendants of the people who invented the snowshoe.

Surviving the Arctic poses the same challenges as living in the desert: finding food, finding shelter, finding water – although most of it is frozen solid. On the advanced courses, you'll travel by dogsled

and learn how to navigate this ice-bound world using the sun, moon and stars.

It's up to you whether you opt for the comparatively balmy months of March and April (average temperature -14°C), or test yourself against the icicle-chill of deep winter.

Pack your warmest thermals for Kangiqsujuaq in Nunavik.

DINE ON DIM SUM WITH A WONTON WOMAN

Duration One to five days ✳ **Cost** HK$1600 per day ✳ **Outcome** Familiarity with woks, cleavers and bamboo steamers ✳ **Where** Hong Kong, China

Can't tell your *siu mai* from your *cheung fan*? Join Hong Kong's answer to the Iron Chef, on an intensive dim-sum cooking course.

WHAT TO EXPECT

'**This isn't** a fancy cooking course for hotel guests. There's no soft music or comfortable sofas.' So says Martha Sherpa, whose battleground – the kitchen – is set up for serious cooking.

Martha teaches both amateur foodies and professional chefs alike, because 'even professionals are beginners when it comes to Chinese cuisine'. She doesn't bow to recipe books or TV shows either (she's been approached for both). Instead, she cracks a mean tea towel, whipping her students into shape over a hot wok, and pointing a gleaming cleaver at anyone taking short cuts with the veg prep.

It will help if you have basic cooking skills, but even if you've never diced a carrot or sliced a shrimp, fear not – everyone in Sherpa's class gets an earful for their perceived lack of skill.

The beauty of this approach is that it feels like a real restaurant kitchen, where it's just you and the dishpig bowing to the grand pooh bah. Along the way, Martha reveals those cooking short cuts that you just don't learn from the recipe books. Oil-free spring rolls? Tick. Perfect wok temperature test? Tick. Chopstick etiquette? Tick.

Martha's class also provides a behind-the-scenes glimpse at Chinese restaurant cuisine – both good and bad aspects.

How it suits you

Dim sum Martha-style would most appeal to an organised – even anally retentive – person, because, like most chefs, Martha keeps a tight rein over her kitchen. Her techniques are military, her cooking implements spotless and her veg diced to perfection. If you lean towards chaotic, focus on the chopstick-eating aspect. If you're likely to get overly emotional when castigated for not holding the wok properly, the kitchen sink is a good place to hide ('dishes are part of a chef's life too').

What you'll get from it

★ **Industry know-how** Martha's commercial background means you get tips on restaurant cooking as well as domestic.
★ **Wok-tastic** Learn the ins and outs of this form of cooking, where a frying pan just doesn't cut it.
★ **Discipline** When Martha says your diced carrots are 'unacceptable' due to slight differentiation in size, it's best just to nod.
★ **Homestyle** Cooking techniques are explained and demonstrated on domestic appliances so you can mimic them at home.

Practical details

Martha Sherpa Cooking School (marthasherpa.com) classes are held in Mong Kok, in Kowloon, Hong Kong. Classes are for four to six people, booked at least seven days in advance.

Other options

In Australia, Sydney's **Urban Graze** (urbangraze.com.au) has a one-day dim sum course. Or try London's **Urban Kitchen** (theurbankitchen.co.uk) 'decadent dim sum' course, coinciding with Chinese New Year. In the US, **Sur La Table** (surlatable.com) and **Hipcooks** (hipcooks.com) offer basic two-hour dim sum classes in various cities.

Doing it at home

When you've mastered the skills of making dim sum, you can make an truly impressive Sunday brunch. You'll fare better with a Chinatown or Asian grocery store nearby to source those tricky ingredients. A kitchenhand will help, too, given the labour-intensive task that lies ahead.

Dumpling gurus let their fingers do the hard work.

JAM ON A DIDGE'
IN ARNHEM LAND

Duration Five days ✳ **Cost** A$2000 ✳ **Outcome** Indigenous spirit, Yolngu language basics and didgeridoo riffs ✳ **Where** Gulkula, Arnhem Land, in Australia's Northern Territory

Learn the meaning behind the dance at the Garma festival.

Celebrate the planet's oldest living culture with the Yolngu people, on the shores of the Gulf of Carpentaria in Arnhem Land.

WHAT TO EXPECT

How often do you get the chance to interact with a 60,000-year-old culture? At their annual Garma Festival, the Yolngu people invite you into their world in Arnhem Land, one of the few corners of the Australian continent where traditional indigenous culture continues to thrive.

Here in Yolngu country, some 2000 people, both black and white, gather each year to celebrate the ancient traditions of Arnhem Land, sharing the knowledge they need to keep their culture strong.

In the Yolngu language, 'garma' means a two-way learning process. Volunteers from the city come here to train the locals in media production or intellectual property, and then sit down for a master class in didgeridoo in the evening.

Getting this close to indigenous Australia's 60,000-year-old culture is a rare experience, and a profound privilege. You'll see elders teaching kids and creating works of art for the international market. Join in the nightly *bungul* traditional dance, wow the crowds with your didgeridoo skills, and embrace the campsite atmosphere that brings everyone together.

Garma is a uniquely immersive cultural experience, offering far more than the tiny taste of indigenous Australia you might find in a museum.

How it suits you

If you're a people person who's not afraid to go where there's no mobile coverage, then Garma is for you. It's remote, it can be very expensive, and when you get there, food and accommodation are basic. But for those who can appreciate the privilege of being part of an encounter with the rich history, spirituality and creativity of the oldest living culture on earth, Garma is a priceless experience.

What you'll get from it

★ **Spirit** You'll learn to understand the deep interconnectedness between Yolngu daily life – whether it's painting, cooking or talking – and Yolngu spirituality.

★ **Smiles** The iridescent grins of the little kids who are here to learn the traditional songs and dances and the irreplaceable spiritual wisdom of their cultures will keep your camera busy – and stay in your heart forever.

★ **Silence** While there's plenty of colour and movement, one thing you won't hear is the ring of a mobile phone.

Practical details

Attending the **Garma Festival** (yyf.com.au) as a cultural tourist isn't cheap, but camping accommodation, meals, transfers and permits are included.

Other options

Garma is the largest festival of indigenous culture in Australia – but you can meet Aboriginal people wherever you go in Australia, and you'll find they're usually more than happy to share their stories and their culture. Keep up your **Yolngu lessons** (www.learnline.cdu.edu.au/yolngustudies) online.

Doing it at home

If you're lucky enough to attend Garma, be sure to take a piece of it back home – whether it's a CD by an emerging local band, a painting to hang on your wall or your own didgeridoo.

SKI WITH STYLE IN TELEMARK, NORWAY

Duration Five days ✳ **Cost** From 590 krone per hour ✳ **Outcome** Find your sense of balance, and exude Scandinavian style and an enviable retro chic on the slopes ✳ **Where** Telemark, southern Norway

How it suits you

You're a detail-oriented person. You're persistent and enjoy mastering difficult skills. You don't feel the need to be quickest down a mountain or the most foolhardy, just the most stylish. You pride yourself on being a bit different, perhaps a bit of a purist, but when you get your groove on there's no stopping you. And yes, admits one telemark instructor, it does suit slightly obsessive personalities.

What you'll get from it

★ **Timing** Can you rub your stomach and pat your head at the same time? Telemark is easier, and when it all comes together, few sensations can beat it.

★ **Grace** A sense of balance is a prerequisite, and a telemark course will help you locate it.

★ **Panache** Telemark isn't about charging downhill a-whoopin' and a-hollerin'. A set of tidy turns is acknowledged not with a high-five but a respectful nod.

★ **Versatility** An ability to use freeheel skis opens swathes of untracked snowy terrain, from the Haute Route of the Alps to North American backcountry.

Practical details

Most ski resorts in Norway provide telemark instruction. **Haukelifjell ski school** (visithaukeli.org) is the closest to Telemark, and can tailor tuition to your requirements.

Other options

North America is a telemark hotbed, with annual telemark festivals, like the Bear Valley Telemark Festival in March, and many resorts offering tuition and equipment rental. Telemark's close cousin, cross-country skiing, draws thousands to Switzerland's impeccably groomed trails, including those around the mountain town of Zuoz in the Engadine valley.

Doing it at home

Count down the months until winter. With your new-found affinity for free-heel skiing you'll be slip-sliding around your snowy neighbourhood. A pair of cross-country skis and boots will see far more use than a downhill set, and ski lifts are no longer required. Plus telemark's fitness boost will benefit your cycling and running while you wait for the first flurry of snowflakes.

WHAT TO EXPECT

Long before rad snowboarders pulled sick airs and skinsuit-clad racers pulled big Gs, there was telemark skiing. Your mission is to perfect your poise, control and balance on two skis, and join Norway's born-again telemarkers on the slopes.

Showcased in the 19th century by Sondre Norheim, who would land ski jumps with arms outstretched and one knee bent, the telemark technique involves making a

Pull on a pair of telemark skis, bend your knees and go back to basics: the original Norwegian skiing style is enjoying a revival, and your new-found elegance will be the talk of the après-ski crowd.

turn by sliding your leading foot back, your body rising as your feet pass, and sinking as your rear knee bends again. The technique is named after the Telemark region, whose gradual slopes offer the perfect territory to pick up the skill.

Telemark skiing is closely related to cross-country, and the addition of skins to the soles of your skis will allow you to shuffle up hills, opening up the wide and wild horizons of ski-touring.

But first you'll have to unlearn your lazy alpine-skiing habits, for in telemark your heel isn't attached to the ski. It requires concentration and timing to master the legwork, keeping your weight evenly distributed between the two skis. But your reward for getting a turn right – the synchronised sliding of your feet back and forth, the rising and falling of your knee – is so addictive that, a century after its heyday, fans of telemark skiing can be found zigzagging down pistes around the world.

And by the end of your intensive tuition you may feel inspired by the challenge of a seven-day traverse of the harsh Hardangervidda plateau, directly north of Telemark.

Telemark turns mean going down on bended knee.

TURN A TREE INTO A
CHAIR IN SOMERSET

Duration Six days ✱ **Cost** £485 ✱ **Outcome** Handy skills, woodland knowledge and an utterly unique piece of furniture ✱ **Where** Bath, UK

Wander the woodlands of Britain to discover the art of green woodworking, and learn to craft an armchair from the trees around you.

WHAT TO EXPECT

Wood shavings shower the floor as you pump the foot treadle that spins your piece of green, unseasoned wood, while you shape it with a carpenter's chisel. You'll never look at a power tool the same way again once you've spent half an hour in the company of a pole lathe.

The art of ancient carpentry is back in vogue thanks to a wave of green woodworking courses in Britain. To get started on making your chair from unseasoned wood – known as bodging in the biz – you'll most likely be given a freshly felled tree and an axe, the aim being to split the wood into useable chunks.

The joy of using unseasoned wood is that it cuts and shapes easily using hand tools, and you'll spend a good chunk of your time seated at a shave horse that acts as both vice and workbench. With your feet operating the clamp, you shape the chair legs by pulling a curved drawknife towards you to sculpt the wood. And you'll investigate other age-old techniques like steam-bending wood and using the natural shrinkage of green timber to create strong, long-lasting joints.

Because you've been following the natural shape of each piece of wood you've worked, while adding your own creative flair, you will leave at the end of the week with a strong, light, functional piece of furniture that is bursting with character.

How it suits you

Practical types will grab the opportunity to discover traditional woodworking techniques, while outdoor enthusiasts will revel in the chance to spend so much time in the middle of a British woodland. This experience also suits outgoing travellers – because you have to work closely with other enthusiasts, you're bound to forge close friendships.

What you'll get from it

★ **Nature therapy** Deep in the woods, surrounded by trees, you'll find yourself absorbed in a way you never imagined possible, squeezing the very last of the daylight to perfect your project.
★ **Wood know-how** Because you're working with the wood's natural shape, you start to develop an instinctive feel for what each piece of wood can achieve.
★ **Practical skills** Don't know how to put up a shelf? This course will reveal hidden depths and unlock your full practical potential. And if you do get stuck there's always an expert on hand to show you the way.

Practical details

There are courses all over the UK. The **Cherry Wood Project** (cherrywoodproject.co.uk) just outside Bath offers two- to nine-day courses in green furniture making, as well as spoon carving and earth-oven building

Other options

Make your own woodworking tools the **Old Time Way** (chuckandpeggypatrick.com), under the watchful eye of a banjo-playing blacksmith in North Carolina. Or build your own Welsh coracle from coppiced hazel poles covered with calico, then launch and paddle it yourself at the **Woodland Skills Centre** (woodlandskillscentre.co.uk) in Wales. In Australia, you can build your own didgeridoo in a weekend, using a naturally termite-hollowed piece of eucalyptus, with **Echo Tree** (echotree.com.au).

Doing it at home

Don't know an oak from an ash? Take time to identify tree species as you explore your local woodland. Collect acorns, conkers and beech nuts to grow your own mini woodland at home and you'll eventually have all the green woodworking materials you need. Get great advice at **Treegrowing** (treegrowing.btcv.org.uk).

Patience plus tools equals
traditional wooden furniture.

MASTER BRAZILIAN
COOKING IN RIO

Duration Four hours ✳ **Cost** R$120 ✳ **Outcome** Dance to the culinary rhythms of Brazil, mix the best caipirinha and be a veritable maestro in the kitchen ✳ **Where** Rio de Janeiro, Brazil

How it suits you

As with all cooking, a rational and organised approach helps you get from point A (dry rice, peppers, onions, raw seafood) to point B (delectable home-cooked Brazilian meal). If you're the type who likes to sit in the back of class and enjoy a good yarn while the teacher extemporises, you'll have a good time whipping up the dishes in the class. Those who focus and take notes will be well armed to re-create the feast at home.

What you'll get from it

★ **Know-how** Whether you're a novice chef or a budding Jamie Oliver, learning to make some key Brazilian dishes will greatly expand your culinary repertoire.

★ **Cultural insight** You'll be surprised by the insights you gain into Brazilian culture – the chef discusses eating customs and the historic roots of the dishes you'll prepare, with a fair dose of humour for good measure.

★ **Bragging rights** 'Here, try this,' you'll say, handing your friends one of the tastiest cocktails they've ever imbibed. 'I learned how to make this, you know, when I was down in Brazil,' you can casually add. 'Care for some more *moqueca*?'

Practical Details

Cook in Rio (cookinrio.com) is based in the neighbourhood of Copacabana in Rio de Janeiro. Four-hour classes are held twice a day Monday through Saturday.

Other Options

Los Angeles-based **Wildwood** (losangelescookingclasses.net) offers a one-day Brazilian BBQ and caipirinha-making class, while **Chef Leticia** (chefleticia.com) gives group and private Brazilian cooking lessons in New York City. In Paraty near Rio, master chef **Yaro Castro Roberts** (thebraziliantable.com) offers evening cooking demonstrations (followed by dinner).

Doing it at Home

Don't waste any time when you get home: organise a dinner party before those cooking skills get rusty. Put on some Brazilian tunes, whip up the cocktails and fire up those dishes still fresh in your mind. Be sure to have plenty of limes and *cachaça* (sugar-cane rum) on hand – a few rounds of caipirinhas will really get the party started.

WHAT TO EXPECT

Take a stroll down Copacabana Beach, detour onto a side street past a peaceful plaza and follow your nose to the aromatic scents of crushed lime, simmering coconut milk and sautéed garlic wafting from the Cook in Rio studio. As one of a small group of students, you'll tie on your apron and delve into the world of Brazilian cookery, putting your hands to work dicing,

Learn how to make a mean *moqueca*, mix a thirst-quenching caipirinha and fire up other Brazilian classics in the *cidade maravilhosa* (marvellous city) of Rio de Janeiro.

chopping, pounding and stirring, then later lifting glass and fork to enjoy the fruits of your labour.

Simone, the garrulous instructor-chef, will make the connections between food and culture come alive as she guides you through the essentials of Brazilian cooking and the fabled relationship between eating and *amor*. After all, cooking in Rio – and in Brazil in general –

isn't strictly about following recipes and measuring out portions. There's a plenty of passion and creativity – call it the samba factor – for which Brazilians are famous. And Simone will show how to access this elemental factor in your own cooking back home.

Of course, you'll also learn how to make some of the classic Brazilian dishes. Choose between

moqueca – a hearty seafood dish with coconut milk and palm oil – or *feijoada*, a pork and black-bean stew (pictured) traditionally consumed on Saturdays; it's so filling, many folks eat little else that day. Both have Afro-Brazilian roots and go brilliantly with a caipirinha, which you'll also learn how to make to perfection (the secret is in the cutting of the limes).

Rio's Sugarloaf mountain looks good enough to eat.

STRUT YOUR STUFF AS A VEGAS POLE DANCER

Duration Four-week course ✳ **Cost** US$149 ✳ **Outcome** Increased fitness, boosted poise and a sexy dance move for every occasion ✳ **Where** Las Vegas, Nevada, US

Shimmy into those Lycra leggings and get down and dirty to learn the art of exotic dancing in Sin City: Las Vegas.

WHAT TO EXPECT

It's true, pole dancing isn't just for strippers and lap dancers any more. These days it's an acrobatic art form, part of the mainstream fitness and dance scene, and a fun way to give your strength and flexibility a workout.

Spinning, holding poses and, yes, gyrating on a floor-to-ceiling pole are a feature of fitness classes and competitions across the US and Australia. Nevertheless, the best place to learn pole dancing is Las Vegas, the home of exotic dancing.

Pole dancing is as common in Vegas as gambling, and dime-a-dozen operations offer quick pole-dancing lessons for bachelorette parties and one-time visitors. But Pole Fitness Studio offers seven levels of classes as well as a full-on exotic dancer course. Have fun, get fit and learn how to dance exotic with a four-week course.

As a student, you'll learn all the essential moves and a stage routine, how to apply make-up and false lashes, and some insights into the psychology of the exotic dance trade. After the four 90-minute classes, you'll strut out of the studio and onto the Strip with an understanding of customer relationships, what kinds of costumes to wear, and how to make your moves look smooth and effortless.

Men are welcome to partake in the studio's co-ed pole dancing classes – and they're not required to wear platform heels.

How it suits you

If you enjoy dance and fitness, the strength and flexibility you'll gain learning new moves will be very satisfying. Performers and artists will appreciate the moves, while exhibitionists will love the attention. Though anyone can learn pole dancing, having a basic level of general fitness will curb frustration and ease the learning curve as you increase your endurance.

What you'll get from it

★ **Smooth moves** Your grace and carriage will be improved by holding pole-dancing's poses.
★ **Overall fitness** The strength and endurance required for pole dancing will tone and shape your body, which is why it's so popular as a fitness class.
★ **Self-confidence** Pole-dancing moves are meant to be sexy, and you'll feel sexier for learning them.
★ **Alternative employment options** If you've discovered your inner Gypsy Rose Lee, Vegas employs plenty of dancers …

Practical details

Pole Fitness Studio (polefitnessstudio.com) offers various pole-dancing classes in Vegas, from beginner to advanced levels, and mixes it up with core strength and co-ed pole classes. The full exotic dance class runs for four weeks, or you can partake in belly dancing and cabaret lessons.

Other options

Founded by a professional ballerina, London's **Pole Dancing School** (poledancingschool.com) focuses on the art form rather than the vocation of pole dancing. As the popularity of pole dancing for fitness increases, so do opportunities for classes. Check your area's gyms for lessons to advance your skills. At **Pole Fitness Australia** (polefitnessaustralia.com), in Brisbane, participants focus on getting fit with pole-dance moves; it also offers classes in burlesque and lap dancing.

Doing it at home

Order a pole for your home and organise a girls' trip to Vegas – or go out and get a job.

Jokes aside, pole dancing is a top-to-pointed-toe workout.

Space tourist Guy Laliberté gets ready to blast off.

Active

COSMONAUT TRAINING
IN MOTHER RUSSIA

Duration One day to four days ✳ **Cost** From US$7000 ✳ **Outcome** The feeling of floating in a zero-gravity environment – the closest thing to going into space itself ✳ **Where** Star City, Moscow, Russia

WHAT TO EXPECT

It's hard to imagine that Star City, once hidden from maps under the veil of Cold War secrecy, is now the setting for commercial space 'experiences'. As long as you're willing to open up your wallet, you can hop on a plane to Moscow and head to the Yuri Gagarin Cosmonaut Training Center at Star City for space training 101.

Experience zero gravity aboard the Illyushin 76 MDK, a plane commonly used for cosmonaut training. NASA dubs such craft 'vomit comets', and it's easy enough to imagine why: a weightless environment is created by taking the plane into a parabolic freefall. If you manage to keep your breakfast down, you'll be taught how to manoeuvre in a zero-G environment. The daring can learn how to spin and somersault.

The faint of heart can instead opt to learn to pilot a spacecraft via simulator training. You will be put behind the 'wheel' of the MIR, Soyuz-TM and even the international space station ... all in a space suit, of course. Complete the cosmonaut experience by undergoing 'hydro' training. You will have seen this in documentaries – astronauts (the Western term) preparing for space-walk missions in a 12 metre-deep water tank (OK, so it's really an aquarium!).

What's next? A trip to space you say? Full Russian cosmonaut training? Sure, it's actually possible ... if you have the savings to shell out $15 to $25 million for the experience.

How it suits you

For the intrepid traveller, you'll be on the forefront of what's to come – space tourism. Not many people can boast of having come this close to actually being in space. Your experience will stand you in good stead when orbital travel becomes a reality. For the scientific mind, the exercise provides fodder for working out the parameters of the perfect weightlessness-inducing parabola.

What you'll get from it

★ **Balance** Moving up and down a cabin while weightless requires an incredible sense of balance. If you don't get it first time, don't worry – the plane will make several parabolic runs.
★ **Eye–hand coordination** You'll come to understand that piloting a spacecraft isn't easy, especially when you're encumbered by a space suit.
★ **Great stories** Top *any* story at a party – just remember to keep tales of projectile vomiting to yourself.

Practical details

Incredible Adventures (incredible-adventures.com) in the US can help book a spot in Star City. You can also try booking via **Best Russian Tour** (bestrussiantour.com).

Other options

Not many countries have space programs so your options are slightly limited. You can undergo 'space flight training' at the **Aurora Aerospace Training Centre** (aurora-aerospace.com) in Florida – don't forget to visit the Kennedy Space Center while you're there.

Doing it at home

We won't mince words: a career as an astronaut isn't easy. The closest you can come to the thrill of space is taking to the skies in a plane or chopper, so consider signing up for the air force or getting a pilot's license. Space tourism you say? Check out **Virgin Galactic** (virgingalactic.com) and start saving up.

Head to Star City in Russia, don a space suit and experience what it's like to float in zero gravity.

SHOUT AND LUNGE LIKE A
WARRIOR IN ROTORUA

Duration Two hours ✳ **Cost** NZ$35 ✳ **Outcome** Shattered inhibitions, a well-exercised tongue and an appreciation of the power of Maori pride ✳ **Where** Rotorua, New Zealand

Child's play: schoolchildren performing on Waitangi Day.

Don't be shy now – stick out your tongue and dance like an All Black! Learn the leaps, lunges and yells of the *haka* in New Zealand's Maori heartland.

WHAT TO EXPECT

Firstly, don't expect to become a Maori in two hours. You can learn 'Ka Mate', the ritual challenge made iconic by the New Zealand All Blacks rugby team; you can learn the words and meaning. But it may take more than a few hours to understand the passion behind the chant.

It's quite extraordinary – and quite terrifying – to watch as your tutor transforms from smiling man to menacing warrior, right before your eyes. But that's what happens when a Maori performs the *haka*. It's not even a war dance – it's the 19th-century celebration song of a chief who managed to hide from the armies on his tail. The first lines, 'Ka mate! Ka mate! Ka ora! Ka ora!', translate as 'It's death! It's death! It's life! It's life!'

You'll be taught the lyrics, along with the actions, which physically retell the story. Hilarity will ensue as you make your first tentative attempts: there's not so much to remember, but there are plenty of inhibitions to forget.

You'll also play dress-up: swirly Maori *mokos* (tattoos) are inked temporarily onto cheeks; regular clothes are swapped for loincloths, wrap-skirts and cloaks made of feathers.

Then it's show time. All that practice culminates in a final run-through, performed in front of a replica *marae* meeting house while the video camera rolls. You die of embarrassment! You live and you love it! This *haka* remains a fine celebration either way.

How it suits you

Extroverts will love learning the *haka* – it'll give them the chance to shout loudest, thrust hardest and wield a large stick. Introverts beware: this is not a dance you can do in half-measures; a nonparticipatory Maori show might be more your thing. Emotional travellers can't help but be moved: it's not so much what the words mean, more their heartfelt delivery – when performing this ritual a Maori holds nothing back. Expect to feel fear and respect in equal parts.

What you'll get from it

★ **Release** Had a bad day? Channelling all that aggression and pent-up emotion into an unbridled *haka* should sort you out.
★ **Liberation** There's no ambivalence with the *haka*: learn to put any self-consciousness aside and make the moves and chants with relish.
★ **The giggles** Two hours of unrestrained ridiculousness (your efforts, not the dance itself)? Fake tattoos, loincloths and wooden clubs? You'll have a blast.
★ **Understanding** You might look silly, but the *haka* is deadly serious. Learn the history behind it, and be mesmerised by your Maori tutor's performance and passion.

Practical details

Haka World (hakaworld.com), based in Rotorua on New Zealand's North Island, runs two-hour 'Ka Mate' *haka* lessons in morning and afternoon sessions. And at the end of the class you can take home a souvenir video!

Other options

Shimmy along to the **Royal Hawaiian Center** (royalhawaiiancenter.com) in Waikiki, which runs a range of cultural classes, including hula lessons. Or join the intertribal dance at a Native American powwow in New Mexico or Alberta – a drumbeat starts and anyone who wants to can take the floor.

Doing it at home

It's not always appropriate to break into a *haka*. But when you're feeling shy or bashful, remember the empowerment of throwing caution to the wind. If you can stamp and yell in a loincloth with strangers, what else might you be able to do?

SHEAR SHEEP IN THE AUSTRALIAN OUTBACK

Duration Five days ✳ **Cost** A$670 ✳ **Outcome** You've wrestled cows, mustered sheep, helped foal a horse and fixed fences – is there anything you can't do? ✳ **Where** Outback New South Wales, Australia

How it suits you

Outfitted in chaps, riding boots and a bush hat, adventurous travellers are stepping into a whole new persona. Cantering through the river on horseback (you were teetering a week ago), brumbies in the distance, lasso in the air ... you'll feel like you're in a movie. The more cool-headed traveller will quickly realise that Mother Nature – and animals – can be capricious on occasion and you'd be toast if you became histrionic. Your pragmatic nature is ideally suited to the realities of life on an outback station.

What you'll get from it

★ **Self-confidence** Overcoming unforeseen challenges and mastering new skills will bolster your self-reliance – now you can take on anything that comes your way.
★ **Perspective** The clean air, manual labour and stunning landscapes have you shuffling your priorities – maybe you don't need those trendy A$300 shoes in Sydney, after all.
★ **Exhilaration** With all this sensory stimulation, all your cells are awakened: you have never felt so alive.
★ **Employability** Now that you've become inseparable from your horse and can work one-on-one with a range of animals, you're considering paying stints.

Practical details

Arrange a station stint with **Jackeroo Jillaroo Australia** (www.jjoz.com.au), which provides full room and board. Note that some activities, such as sheep shearing, are seasonal.

Other options

In the UK, try light bushcraft with a farmstay at **Coldharbour Cottage** (coldharbourcottage.co.uk) or search **Farmstay UK** (farmstay.co.uk). Or try the open skies in Nebraska at **1+1 Ranch** (1plus1ranch.com) in the USA, and anything from a High Andes Cattle Drive to African ranch stays and other global riding adventures with **Unicorn Trails** (unicorntrails.com).

Doing it at home

Research opportunities to visit working farms and check out farmers markets in your area where you can meet and support local producers. Pining for a pony? Consider volunteering at a horse stable.

WHAT TO EXPECT

Good thing you sprung for that Akubra hat at the airport – you're seeing it has a purpose under the glorious blazing sun out here on the station. Now 10am, and a couple of hours since you tucked into a hearty, home-grown breakfast, you're straddled atop a horse and focused on the cattle around you, some of which have

Get an authentic taste of the Australian bush by learning the ropes as a cowboy or cowgirl on a working sheep and cattle station.

minds of their own. The dog trotting at your side will help with that. After your crash course in horsemanship, you can feel the bush life already seeping into your soul.

You're covering a lot of ground at jackeroo school – in more ways than one. You quickly became acquainted with the mechanics of your wrist as you learn how to handle a whip, lasso and various farm implements. You're speaking a whole new vocabulary (is that an Aussie accent?) after lessons in mustering and crutching, drenching and calf-throwing. Multitasking is a real survival skill out here, too, and you're learning just how outback Aussies deal with bushfires and mobs of kangaroos.

If it were all 'work', Jack and Jill would be pretty dull and that's definitely not the Aussie way – in the evenings under that expansive, star-lit sky, you're kicking back with a coldie and swapping stories with your mates, feeling very much at home on this range.

Mustering sheep for shearing is hot work. Time for a cold beer.

HEAL YOURSELF WITH
HERBS IN KERALA

Duration From one month ✳ **Cost** €420 per one-month course ✳ **Outcome** Healing wisdom, knowing how to give an oil massage and a new way of looking at life ✳ **Where** Kerala, South India

A relaxing herb-infused bath is part of Ayurveda's detoxification process.

Healing massages, herbal compresses, scented oils – these are just a few of the things you'll encounter when you study ayurvedic medicine in Kerala.

WHAT TO EXPECT

When the monkey god Hanuman lopped the top off a mountain to bring a healing herb to Lord Rama, he was following a tradition as old as the Indian hills. Drawing on medicinal plants that grow wild from the plains to the high Himalaya, ayurveda (Indian herbal medicine) has been practised in the subcontinent for at least 3500 years. That's plenty of time to refine the art of imparting this wisdom to willing students.

Studying ayurveda in India is up there with learning acupuncture in China, and the same rules apply – don't expect to be able to pack in the day job after a single course of study. After all, would you go to a doctor who had only one month of med school under their belt? On the other hand, if you like the idea of starting your mornings with yoga stretches and spending the day learning how to administer ayurvedic oil massages and the correct technique of *shirodhara* (dripping oil therapy), then this could be the experience for you.

Beach-fronted Kannur, a leafy provincial town on the north Kerala coast, is the capital of ayurvedic study in South India. At reputable schools here, ayurveda is woven into the fabric of each day; even meals are prepared according to ayurvedic principles. In between hands-on practical sessions, you'll delve into ancient philosophical principles that could change the way you look at the universe. That's something to take home, alongside a new-found knowledge of healing herbal therapies.

How it suits you

Spiritual travellers will thrive on a course founded on changing the way you look at the world, but anyone can benefit from the practical aspects of ayurveda. If you don't go in for philosophy, you could always put yourself on the receiving end of ayurvedic treatments in Kerala's idyllic spas. Only serious students should pursue the practice of *panchakrama*, a vigorous detox therapy using everything from enemas to leeches.

What you'll get from it

★ **Knowledge** Even if you learn only a tiny fraction of ayurvedic herbal lore, it could open the door to a new way of living.
★ **Skills** We're not saying you can set up as a therapist overnight, but you can certainly revolutionise the way you unwind at home.
★ **Wellbeing** If nothing else, a vegetarian diet, fruit lunches and abstinence from Western vices like smoking and alcohol will help clear your system.

Practical details

Some Kannur schools seem more interested in money than healing, but **PVA Ayurvedic Hospital** (ayurvedaacharya. com) has a good teacher-to-student ratio and a reputable medic at the helm. Courses run monthly year-round.

Other options

Pack your acupuncture needles and set off to study traditional Chinese medicine at the **China Beijing International Acupuncture Training Centre** (www.cbiatc.com), learn traditional medicine from Tibetan lamas in the Indian Buddhist enclaves of Dharamsala and Leh through the **Men-tsee-khang Cultural Centre** (men-tsee-khang.org) or study ancient Thai massage at the **Wat Po Thai Traditional Medical School** (watpomassage.com; see p36-37) in Bangkok.

Doing it at home

Ayurvedic treatments are easy to find at any spa worth its bath salts. To move your own knowledge of ayurveda forward, read broadly around the subject and stock up on herbs from a recognised ayurvedic dealer.

WALK THE WINGS OF A BIPLANE IN BRITAIN

Duration One hour ✳ **Cost** £400 to £500 ✳ **Outcome** Old-world class, bags of confidence and heaps of mystique ✳ **Where** England, UK

Feel the wind and adrenalin whip through you with every dive and 'loop the loop' as you wing walk on top of a biplane.

WHAT TO EXPECT

Your heart is already racing and you're still on the ground! Soon, though, you'll be hurtling through the air at up to 215kph.

Your wing-walking instructor helps you clamber onto the biplane's top pair of glossy wings, then straps you standing against a pole with a seatbelt harness around your shoulders and waist. Don't worry: the centre clip buckles down – once locked, it can't accidentally come loose.

The pilot can see you at all times, but not hear you, so you need to know the hand signals. One arm up means *yes*. Very few people use two thumbs down, which means *I'm really not happy – please land*, but it's good to know!

After 45 minutes of training, it's show time. The plane takes off and you get a clear view of the countryside below you on your 10-minute flight. You can't turn your head because the air catches in your mouth, but you raise both your arms, which means *really go for it!* so the pilot weaves the plane to give you a panoramic view of the green fields unfolding below. Up so high, fear turns into exhilaration, and the white noise of the whirling plane and the air blasting onto your face is oddly soothing.

Then the plane swoops towards the ground, where your friends and family snap photos of their daredevil star zipping by with a wide grin, despite a snot-splattered face.

How it suits you

Flying on the exterior of a plane gives adrenalin junkies a dose of heights and speed. If bungee jumping and sky diving have lost their edge, this could be your new high. Wing walking has been performed since the 1920s, so travellers with a love of history will get a taste for the old aviation days.

What you'll get from it

★ **High** The adrenalin will make your spirits soar. Wing walking is exhilarating and teaches you to make the most of the moment.

★ **Confidence** Even if wing walking terrifies you at first, the satisfaction of having conquered your fears will get the happy endorphins pumping. Learning how to take control of your fears is a lifelong skill.

★ **A sense of history** Wing walking really took off in the US after WWI, with pilots performing hand stands and other stunts on the wings. The UK eagerly took up the plane revolution in the early days of aviation, making it a history-rich place to fly.

Practical details

Wing Walk Displays (wingwalkdisplays.co.uk) has two locations in England – one in Berkshire and one near York. Protective clothing is provided. Classes run from April to October. You can invite up to 50 spectators to come and cheer you on.

Other options

Wing walking is effectively banned for amateurs in the US, but performers exist, such as **Bob Essell Airshows** (bobessellairshows.com) in Ohio, the state where the Wright Brothers built the first plane.

Doing it at home

Now that you're back on land, do you miss feeling the wind rushing in your face? Feel it again on solid ground with a motorbike ride. Wing walking is better in figure-hugging outfits and with theatrics, so will you use these skills in dance or designing costumes? Or take the hand stands to a park for fitness?

Once you've mastered wing-walking,
you will never fear anything ever again.

CRAFT CLAY POTS IN CAPPADOCIA

Duration Eight hours ✳ **Cost** From €53 ✳ **Outcome** Meet a Turkish hair fetishist and craft your own Cappadocian pottery ✳ **Where** Avanos, Cappadocia, Turkey

How it suits you

This is an adventure no art lover should miss, a tactile plunge into a destination most people only appreciate through photos. Your full-day introduction to all things clay will catch your fancy whether you're practised in the sculptural arts, devoted to the history that makes them so exciting or happy to dabble in a little of both. Come prepared to be social, to shake the locals' calloused hands and then start toughening up your own.

What you'll get from it

★ **Pottery facts** For millennia, clay containers have stored wine and food, terracotta pots have been used for cooking, and the deceased have even been buried in clay coffins. You'll leave Galip's workshop with an appreciation of pottery's part in history.

★ **Art appreciation** Learn the techniques, decorative motifs and colours that have made Avanos' earthenware famous. Some special designs have been used for centuries by families like Galip's.

★ **Tall tales** Where else can you see 16,000 locks of hair in a museum?

Practical details

Your private Cappadocia pottery pilgrimage can be booked through **Gunyah** (gunyah.com, click on Turkey) year-round for between two and six people.

Other options

Classes in ceramic arts, including kick-wheel pottery – or the more contemporary motor-driven equivalent – are available all across the globe. Good places to start a search are the **Archie Bray Foundation** (archiebray.org) and **International Ceramics Directory** (ceramics-directory.com).

Doing it at home

If you don't own your own potter's wheel, you can often rent access to one in a local arts and craft centre, where you can also use the paint, finishing tools and the kiln for firing. The rest is up to you, your vision and your touch – the potter's essentials.

WHAT TO EXPECT

Meet Chez Galip, a sixth-generation master potter clad in pug-stained *şalvar* (Turkish baggy trousers). For decades, Galip has been leading his town's revival as a centre for high-quality earthenware in Cappadocia.

Getting grit under your fingernails as you kick-spin a potter's wheel and give shape to a lifeless lump of clay is very gratifying, and Galip clearly feels the same way. In his large cave-house, typical of this part of

Using clay dredged from a nearby river and inspiration from a local master ceramicist, kick-spin your own souvenir into gear on a traditional potter's wheel.

Turkey, Galip maintains a workshop and gallery where he proudly throws, fires and displays his intricately designed and boldly coloured ceramics. This is also where he welcomes visitors like you to watch demonstrations and participate in kick-wheel classes.

Your encounter with Galip caps a day devoted to the history and art of pottery. You will already have travelled to the Nevşehir Museum to behold the oldest pottery in Cappadocia; stopped for tea near a monument to potters and at a bridge over the Kızılırmak (Red River), which contributes its mineral-rich mud to the region; settled into a lunch of *testi kebap*, a traditional dish cooked in a clay pot; and explored the country's biggest private underground pottery cave-museum.

But it's your time with Galip that will stay with you longest, not just because of his infectious enthusiasm and the homemade wine he serves. During a personal kick-wheel demonstration, you'll follow his lead and craft your own ceramic souvenir.

One eccentric bonus: check out Galip's Hair Museum, with its locks lovingly shorn from 16,000 women (don't ask why).

Take your inspiration from the natural wonders of Love Valley near Goreme.

SHAKE IT LIKE A VAHINE IN FRENCH POLYNESIA

Duration From one month ✳ **Cost** From 6500 Pacific francs ✳ **Outcome** Hip and pelvis work-out, informal French lessons and new Tahitian friends ✳ **Where** Tahiti, French Polynesia

Your hips may never move at 1000rpm like the pros, but take up Tahitian dance and you'll learn to wiggle your booty with style.

WHAT TO EXPECT

All Polynesian countries have a hip-swaying style of traditional dance but Tahiti's is arguably the fastest, sexiest and most theatrical. Get ready to shimmy and sway with everyone from French expats to retired Tahitian ladies!

Even if your hips are as supple as a tin man's, and you speak no more than three words of French, a smile and a friendly attitude will have you swaying along with your fellow classmates, many of whom have been hitting the dance floor for years and can act as de facto teachers.

Classes begin with a few minutes of stretching, followed by some warm-ups. Fast, percussion-heavy Tahitian music blares over the stereo as you work on your *ueue,* the signature circular hip movement that provides the base of the dance. Then prepare to sweat as you and your fellow students (numbering five to 50, depending on the class) join in the formation of several lines of dancers. Each dancer takes their turn to shimmy across the floor, mastering different versions of the hip sway.

Certain moves such as the *afata* ('hips like a box') are complex, with the pelvis moving in several directions. You'll learn each move in slow motion before speeding it up. The choreography is equally detailed, with hand gestures that tell a story.

The last half of the class is dedicated to learning the choreography of a dance you'll perform with the group if you stick around long enough (five to nine months!). The workout finishes with slow stretches to soft ukulele music.

Although Tahitian dance classes are oriented towards female participants, men are more than welcome to join in.

How it suits you

Rational types will love figuring out the mechanics of Tahitian dance. If you're more spontaneous, it's as easy to learn the moves by surrendering yourself to the music and letting your body learn the details on its own.

What you'll get from it

★ **A workout** Think legs, abs and arms with all the cardio you can handle, but the classes are so fun you'll enjoy sweating them out.
★ **Grace** Mastering the body, feeling sexy and standing tall is a part of what makes Tahitian women so lovely – a little island charm in your step is the best souvenir to bring home.
★ **Cultural connection** You can't dance in a group without making a few friends, plus you'll get in on all the islander laughter and gossip.

Practical details

Heirani Salmon (call her on (+689) 706 997) has excellent dance studios in Taravao and, closer to Papeete, in Punuaaia. The best time to join up is late August, when the academic school year begins, but of course you can learn any time of year. Courses usually run for one hour, twice a week, and are held in small dance studios with parquet floors. Wear a sports bra and a *pareu* (sarong), bring a big bottle of water and you're ready to rock.

Other options

The biggest concentration of Tahitian dance schools is found on Tahiti and Moorea. You can sign up for classes in France, Hawaii and elsewhere, and other South Pacific nations such as Samoa, Tonga and Rarotonga also have their own dance traditions.

Doing It at home

Your grass skirt and coconut bra will liven up any fancy dress party, and busting those hip rolls will make you look and feel like Shakira on the dance floor. You'll put your Robot and Pepper-grinding friends to shame.

With the dance talents you perfected on Tahiti you'll be able to out-booty Beyonce any day of the week.

Nothing brings the Colosseum to life like clutching a sword and pretending you're a gladiator.

Active

GRAPPLE WITH GLADIATORS IN ROME

Duration Two hours ❋ **Cost** €55 to €100 ❋ **Outcome** Choose your favourite helmet, brush up on your Roman history and get the lowdown on fencing gladiator-style ❋ **Where** Rome, Italy

Try on a helmet, wield your shield and sword, and feel your imagination go into overload as you enter the arena, decked out like Russell Crowe from *Gladiator*. Will it be thumbs up or thumbs down?

Gruppo Storico Romana is a historical re-enactment group in Rome, who, as well as organising regular costumed events, run 'Gladiator for a Day' courses. Set in the pea-green countryside that surrounds the ancient Roman road Via Appia Antica, their headquarters consist of a Roman fortress, museum and arena, all dedicated to giving visitors an insight into gladiatorial life in the days of Imperial Rome.

You'll start your lesson in the museum, which contains armour and information on the various types of ancient Roman gladiators. The burly English-speaking teacher will explain the nuances of combat and provide some background on the different types of warriors. Here you'll have a chance to try on helmets and shields, choosing from models worn from the 4th century BC to the 2nd century AD.

With images of blood-lusting crowds swirling in your mind, it's time to enter the gladiatorial arena. Equipped with a wooden *rudis* (practice sword), you'll do battle with a partner, practising the rhythmic patterns of the fight as your teacher explains defensive and attacking gladiatorial combat moves. If you show the skill to succeed, your teacher may even suggest you try out the much more dangerous *gladius* (a metal weapon).

At the end you'll receive a certificate that testifies to your newly acquired gladiatorial skills – an asset on any CV or resumé.

How it suits you

Becoming a gladiator for a day, or just a few hours, will suit history-lovers and those who like to try things out for themselves. If you like to get stuck into the experience of history, rather than observing its relics in a glass case, being a Gladiator for the Day is for you.

What you'll get from it

★ **Rhythm** The art of gladiatorial combat follows surprisingly formal patterns.
★ **Knowledge** This is an exhilarating way to bring history to life, fighting in a sun-baked arena so close to the ruins of ancient Rome.
★ **Sense of the absurd** It's rather thrillingly absurd to learn to fight as gladiators did thousands of years ago.

Practical details

The lessons take place at the **Gruppo Scuola Roma** (gsr-roma.com) headquarters, south of Rome on Via Appia Antica. Lessons are available on request (to those aged seven and upwards) and may be conducted privately or with larger groups.

Other options

At the **Royal Armouries** (www.royalarmouries.org) in Leeds, you can visit the crossbow-shooting gallery and try out your skills. Study European fencing arts, including duelling with sabres and rapiers, at New York's **Martinez Academy of Arms** (martinez-destreza.com/school), or visit the **Joust School** (www.jousting.co.nz) in New Zealand to learn joust and weapons skills.

Doing it at home

It's tricky to see how you might apply your new-found skills in modern life without being arrested. However, your gladiatorial certification may be the perfect trigger for organising a Roman-themed fancy-dress party, with demonstrations. If you have school-age children who're interested in Roman history, they'll love learning to battle it out like a gladiator. In fact dressing up like a gladiator brings Roman history furiously and excitingly to life for participants of any age.

Channel your inner Spartacus for the most inspirational history lesson you're ever likely to have, as you learn to battle it out like the professional gladiators of 2000 years ago.

CARVE YOUR OWN MAORI
ART IN NEW ZEALAND

Duration One day ✴ **Cost** NZ$79 ✴ **Outcome** Express your creativity, work with your hands and leave with a treasure to cherish or give to a loved one ✴ **Where** Nelson, New Zealand

Learn to carve a pendant from bone and create your own unique piece of Maori art in New Zealand's South Island.

WHAT TO EXPECT

Bone pendants are one of the great *taonga* (treasured possessions) of Maori culture, an art form blending traditional craft with personal history. You can carve your own treasured possession at a workshop in Nelson.

Workshops are run in small groups so there's plenty of personal guidance. You'll learn iconic Maori designs such as *hei matau* (fish hook), *hei tiki* (human form) and *hei koru* (unfurling fern frond). As Maori *whakairo* (carving) preserves traditional knowledge and heritage, such as *whakapapa* (lineage) and mythology, the stories behind these designs are as fascinating as the pieces are beautiful.

You'll begin by drawing your design, either a traditional Maori symbol, or another tradition such as Celtic or Egyptian. Once your initial design is settled, a piece of beef shin-bone – known for its ivory-like qualities – is crudely shaped with brute tools such as the fretsaw, bench-grinder and drill. Then it's down to files, sandpaper and elbow grease, as the roughly hewn piece is honed. Soon it emerges smooth and finely shaped: your very own pendant.

The bone changes colour as it absorbs oils from the wearer's skin; Maori believe this imbues the pendant with human spirit. If you're going to make a gift of your carving to a loved one, it is traditional to wear the piece for a while so that some of your *mauri* (spirit) is shared with them, too.

How it suits you

If you're artistic and good with your hands, you'll probably get into the bone zone quite quickly. However, the beauty of a carving workshop is that anyone can give it a go. In fact, it's often those students with the least experience, or those who believe they have few creative talents, who find bone carving a particularly satisfying voyage of discovery. 'I never thought my scribbling could turn into something so beautiful and well crafted,' said one workshop attendee.

What you'll get from it

★ **Insight** Traditional Maori carving has stories to tell, and here is a chance to hear some of them.
★ **Inspiration** Discover the artist within – it might be a lot closer to the surface than you think.
★ **Connection** Come down to earth and explore an art that has resonated throughout the ages.
★ **Instant heirloom** You'll leave with a treasure made with your own hands and with so much more meaning than something bought from a shop.
★ **Mauri spirit** Between engaging your imagination, shaping your vision and the meditative process of polishing your piece, this endeavour will be good for the soul.

Practical details

Full-day workshops are held year-round by **Stephan the Bone Carver** (carvingbone.co.nz) in a backyard studio near Tahunanui Beach, Nelson. Bookings are required, and local pick-up is available.

Other options

Near Milton Abbas in Dorset, UK, **Flux 'n' Flame** (fluxnflame.co.uk) runs jewellery-making courses at a countryside workshop. In Australia, the **Jewellery School** (jewel-school.com) at Coolum Beach, Queensland, has gold- and silver-smithing weekend courses for beginners.

Doing it at home

Get your hands on some beef bone and your bone-carving journey can continue. Stephan's DVD series – *The Foundation* and *The Master Class* – provides ample guidance and an extended range of techniques to explore at home.

Whether you copy a traditional design or develop your own, the process of bone carving is intensely personal.

OLÉ! GAIN FLAMENCO STYLE IN SEVILLE

Duration As long as it takes ✳ **Cost** From €10 per lesson ✳ **Outcome** Foot-stomping awesomeness, the key to Seville's character and a love of frills ✳ **Where** Seville, Spain

How it suits you

Flamenco is deeply, powerfully expressive, and while it naturally suits extroverts, a flamenco alter-ego can do wonders for anyone who has trouble finding an outlet for their feelings of crazed passion, violent rage and desperate sorrow. Most of all, it's perfect for anyone who yearns to liven things up by donning a frilly skirt, stamping their feet, waving their arms and shouting 'Olé!'

What you'll get from it

★ **Rhythm** The complex *compas,* or rhythms, are tricky to get your head around, but they're the heart of flamenco's sophistication.
★ **Therapy** There's nothing like a good few hours of foot-pounding to clear your head.
★ **Muscles** You'll know what we're talking about after your first lesson. Flamenco works everything from the toes to the fingertips, not to mention the facial muscles you need for all that intense frowning.
★ **Duende** The spirit of flamenco can't be described, only felt and expressed.

Practical details

Beginners can dip their toe in with a quick 20-minute class at Seville's **Flamenco Museum** (museoflamenco.com), where the daily shows are also worthwhile. The fully committed can enrol in a summer intensive or year-long course at the **Fundación Cristina Heeren** (flamencoheeren.com).

Other options

There are very fine flamenco schools throughout Spain and, in fact, all over the world. Indeed, such is the universal appeal of the dance that there are more flamenco schools in Japan than there are in Spain.

Doing it at home

When your friends say they're 'going out dancing', they mean shifting nonchalantly from one foot to another. Just down a few *vino tintos*, get up on the table and give them the biggest *zapateo* you've got: a flamenca is never a wallflower. To order the frilly gear, try **Flamenco World** (flamenco-world.com).

WHAT TO EXPECT

Flamenco lurks around every corner in Seville – at the *peñas* (flamenco performances – try Casa de la Memoria de Al-Andalus, La Carbonería and Los Gallos for some of the best); in the streets of the old gypsy barrio Triana; and in the city's souvenir stores, where spotted frilly aprons hang in every doorway.

Try dancing the flamenco, though, and you'll soon discover it's a tough thing to

Flamenco was born in the gypsy *barrios* of Andalusia, so head to Seville to stamp your feet, swirl your skirts and stir up the fiery passion of the dance that's caught fire around the world.

pull off. The *bailaora* (dancer) is both musician and dancer, her feet beating complex and varied staccato rhythms while her languid arms and fingers move expressively. Dance steps, instruments (guitar, *cajón* and *palmas*, or clapping hands) and, most importantly, songs combine to involve the entire person – you need strong legs, a focused mind that understands the complex rhythms, graceful and

flexible arms, and a sensitivity to the dark *duende*: that elusive notion at the heart of Andalusian culture, whose spirit fills the plays and poems of Federico García Lorca and cries out at Seville's many *peñas*.

Experts are divided on flamenco's exact heritage. The dance is thought to mix the music of the Romani people with the sounds of North Africa, while others argue that its

roots extend back to Persian song, the classical orchestras of the Islamic Empire, the songs of the Jewish synagogues or the Byzantine chants of Visigothic churches.

Whatever its origins, one thing's for sure: flamenco is a unique form of artistic expression, whose irrepressible rhythm and anguished melodies provide Spain's signature soundtrack.

As a *flamenca* it is your right to always look fabulous and colourful, and out-perform everyone else in sight.

DYE TRADITIONAL
DESIGNS IN MALI

Duration Two days ✳ **Cost** From US$180 ✳ **Outcome** Your own hand-dyed *bògòlan* mudcloth souvenir, tips for washing clothes in the river and a new-found respect for mud ✳ **Where** Djenné, Mali

As you're rinsing off your creation the locals will be quick to inform you if you've made the best use of your mud.

Exercise your artistic fancy and grasp the cultural importance of Mali's natural materials and age-old techniques, then make your vision a mudcloth reality.

WHAT TO EXPECT

The ancient town of Djenné is well versed in the uses of mud – its famous Great Mosque is a case in point, an impressive structure built entirely out of the stuff. In fact, Djenné is considered one of the world's top adobe towns – a plaudit that helped it earn World Heritage Site status – so where else would you learn how to create *bògòlan*, handmade cloth dyed with special mud?

A two-day *bògòlanfini* experience is a hands-on workshop in the method behind the madness of creating Mali's quintessential *bògòlan* (meaning 'made from mud' in Bambara, Mali's main language).

The *bògòlan* classes cover the background and the basics, including a look at Bambara culture, the history and traditions of the textile, and the natural and artisanal techniques used to create it – the plants, their treatment and their application in the preparation and painting of the cloth.

You'll also witness weaving demonstrations, then get to paint your own freestyle motifs onto cotton cloth. If you're inspired by the traditional patterns you'll see demonstrated, you might want to have a go at replicating the blacksmith caste's *forgeron* pattern. When you're happy with the result, head to the river to wash your finished cloth with the locals.

A side trip is also made to nearby Diabolo village to observe the *bògòlan* methods in action.

How It suits you

Whether you stick to traditional patterns or come up with your own, the design and decorative processes require real creativity – you'll need to apply mud by using a toothbrush, painting freehand or using stencils. Travellers with an appreciation of history will also enjoy the experience, which delves into Malian Bambara culture and tradition.

What you'll get from it

★ **Art appreciation** Djenné and the surrounding villages are highly regarded for the quality of their *bògòlan* and their use of totally organic methods.

★ **Community connection** The river excursion to wash the decorated fabric and dry it in the sun puts you right next to the villagers, who are busy laundering their clothes and tempering their curiosity about you.

★ **Warm glow** If you're into spending responsibly, your fee will help fund small projects in health, culture and education in the Djenné area.

Practical details

This private, two-day *bògòlan* workshop, including an overnight in a mud-built hotel and the trip to Diabolo, is bookable year-round at **Gunyah** (gunyah.com, click on Mali and 'Cultural Heritage Breaks'). No previous experience with textiles is required.

Other options

Batik art workshops, using wax and dye, involve similar methods and are widely found in North America through **Modern Batik Art Workshops** (modernbatikartworkshops.com), in the UK via the **Batik Guild** (batikguild.org.uk) and elsewhere. Quilting is arguably the cultural equivalent of *bògòlan* in North America; check out **American Quilter** (americanquilter.com).

Doing it at home

At home, it won't be easy to source local variants of the Malian base products used in making a traditional *bògòlan,* especially the cotton cloth, the bark or leaves needed for the red or yellow dye, and the mud that typically comes from the Niger River itself. If nothing else, the patterns you learn can be used in other art and craft projects.

FARM PRIZE PUMPKINS IN SOUTH KOREA

Duration One week ✳ **Cost** Willing Workers on Organic Farms (WWOOF) membership ✳ **Outcome** Calloused hands, agricultural skills and lungfuls of country air ✳ **Where** South Korea

Learn the ins-and-outs of faming organic pumpkins in South Korea, the land of the morning calm.

WHAT TO EXPECT

It's simple really. Sign up as a member of the Willing Workers on Organic Farms. Fly to South Korea and trade your time and labour on a modest organic pumpkin farm in return for food and lodging. Along the way, pick up new skills, a better understanding of how the land works and learn about farming practices in Korea. No matter how long your stay – a week or two months – the routine will quickly establish itself.

Depending on when you go, you might be involved in anything from the seeding of fields and their watering and tending to the harvesting and packing of pumpkins. Of course, if pumpkins don't rock your world there are a whole host of other types of farms to work on. The setting itself is surprisingly idyllic: not many people realise that the inner heart of South Korea is lush and beautiful.

A quick trawl across blogs and forums reveals many great encounters with South Korean farmers. You'll often be housed in the spare bedroom in the farmer's house, and fed home-cooked Korean cuisine. Repay your hosts' kindness by spending time chatting and sharing about your life back home – as much as you're interested in Korean culture, the locals will be keen to hear about your part of the world.

How it suits you

The cultural traveller will enjoy travelling and working in rural, not-often-seen parts of Korea. Far from the tourist scrum of Jeju-Do or the hustle and bustle of Seoul, these stints will take you into the beautiful beating agricultural heart of the land. The do-er will relish spending time engaging with local work routines and (literally) getting their hands dirty on a daily basis.

What you'll get from it

★ **Culture** You'll be living and working in close proximity to locals – you'll learn local phrases and experience their life and culture firsthand.
★ **Great stories** Add to the fantastic blog posts about the WWOOF experience in South Korea – you'll be able to shed light on a part of Korea people aren't often familiar with, and everyone loves a good yarn.
★ **Green fingers** You'll be able to tell secateurs from scissors, weeds from shoots and leave with the skills to start and maintain a thriving garden of your own.

Practical details

You'll need to pay for membership to the Korean branch of **WWOOF** (koreawwoof.com). Membership gets you an handbook (in English) detailing all the farms participating in the scheme. Decide which farm you'd like to stay at a month in advance, and let the organisers set it all up.

Other options

WWOOF is big internationally, with over a thousand organic WWOOF farms in **Australia** (wwoof.com.au) and the **US** (wwoofusa.org). The WWOOF network also extends to Europe, Latin America and Africa. Check out the **WWOOF** website (wwoof.org) for more international links.

Doing it at home

Take your new-found skills and turn your backyard into a sustainable vegetable farm. The basics of farming are similar, so if you can tend to organic pumpkins you can apply the same knowledge to herbs (rosemary, sage, mint etc) and other vegetables (tomatoes, potatoes). And when you reap your first harvest, throw a barbecue to celebrate. What's next? A stall at the local farmers market?

WWOOFing allows travellers to learn farming secrets from cultures around the world.

Canyonlands National Park – a stunning setting in which to practise your new desert survival skills.

UNEARTH YOUR INNER
CAVEMAN IN UTAH

Duration Seven to 28 days ✳ **Cost** From US$1375 ✳ **Outcome** The ability to hunt for food and start a fire with two sticks – you never know when that could come in handy! ✳ **Where** Southern Utah, US

A dry wind blows over the parched canyons, as the sun beats down like a jackhammer and vultures circle overhead. Somewhere out there in the wilderness is food, water and shelter, but you have to find it. This scary scenario is the premise of a survival course in the badlands of southern Utah.

If you can't last five minutes without your BlackBerry, this probably isn't for you. But if the idea of being dropped into the desert with nothing but your wits to keep you alive stimulates your sense of adventure, it could be the experience of a lifetime.

Taking inspiration from the Pueblo Indians, the Boulder Outdoor Survival School was founded as the antidote to modern living. If you can survive with nothing more than what you can make with your own hands, the logic goes, who needs anything else? On the hunter-gatherer course, you'll learn to find water, identify medicinal plants, hunt your own dinner, even make your own clothes and spears from plants and rocks.

It won't be easy – participants can expect to lose a couple of kilos from the rigours of desert living. The good news is you don't have to go it alone. Would-be survivors head out into the desert in small groups and learn to live as a tribe, sharing tasks and responsibilities.

Human beings managed to live like this for 200,000 years, so what's stopping you?

How it suits you

If you relish adventure, learning to survive in the desert is about as adventurous as you can get. The physical, mental and emotional challenges can be immense – even hardened outdoor enthusiasts will find themselves tested to breaking point. The trade-off is a set of skills that will set you up for a lifetime, and the chance to find out what you are really made of.

What you'll get from it

- ★ **Self-reliance** You'll never find out if you have what it takes to survive unless you put yourself in a situation where you have to!
- ★ **Knowledge** It wasn't so long ago that every human being knew how to find water and hunt for food – now you will too.
- ★ **Being prepared** You may never need to use your extreme survival skills, but should civilisation crumble, at least you'll know you can get by.
- ★ **Inner strength** Pitting yourself against the desert will teach you as much about yourself as about the rocks and sand.

Practical details

Boulder Outdoor Survival School (boss-inc.com) runs survival courses lasting seven, 14 or 28 days. Courses start on fixed dates from May to September.

Other options

Swap deserts for snow and ice on a subzero survival course at the **Nunavik Arctic Survival Training Centre** (nastc. ca; see p112-113), or head to the Brazilian rainforest to learn the skills of jungle survival from native guides through **Bushmasters** (bushmasters.co.uk). To learn how to survive in a post-Apocalyptic world, join an urban survival course in the American Midwest.

Doing it at home

Hunting with a homemade bow and arrow might raise a few eyebrows in the suburbs, but you could always use your new-found survival skills on a wilderness camping trip. Start with foraging and building shelters before you move to spear-fishing in the local park!

Do you have what it takes to survive in the desert with nothing but a knife, a blanket and a poncho? Find out on a no-holds-barred survival course in the badlands of Utah.

COOK UP A FEAST FIT FOR A PASHA IN JORDAN

Duration Morning, afternoon or evening sessions ✳ **Cost** From 30 dinar per class ✳ **Outcome** Learn how to infuse dinner parties with the exotic flavours of the souq ✳ **Where** Amman, Jordan

How it suits you

For the leader of the gourmet dinner party pack, this is the Levantine notch-on-the-belt you've been waiting for. Culture vultures will want to grab this opportunity to explore Arab culture through its cuisine – nothing expresses the unique blend of influences that have stomped their path through this region like the food does.

What you'll get from it

★ **Technique** Empowered by the kitchen methods of the Middle Eastern cook, the perfect Levantine menu is now yours to create.

★ **Appreciation for detail** In a world of 30-minute dishes and one-pot meals, it's a luxury to spend some serious time in front of the stove, stirring and tasting to perfection.

★ **Inspiration** Didn't know what tahini was before? Never cooked with yoghurt? Well now that you do, take this new-found knowledge away and experiment to your culinary imagination's limit.

Practical details

Beit Sitti (beitsittijo.com) hosts daily cooking lessons in downtown Amman. Choose from a brunch, lunch or dinner itinerary, and select the menu you'd like to cook.

Other options

In England, food-writer **Anissa Heleu** (anissas.com) runs classes focused on Levantine-inspired dishes from her London kitchen. In Australia, globe-trotting chef **Elise Pascoe** (cookingschool.com.au) offers Middle Eastern cooking classes near Kiama in New South Wales. Over in the US, Syrian chef **Ahmad Yasin** (yasinculinary.com) takes you through your Arab cookery paces at his school in Massachusetts.

Doing it at home

Chuck on some music by Fairuz to set the mood, dust off that shisha pipe you bought in the souq, and transport your friends to the deserts and mountains of the Middle East with a spread of Levantine favourites that would make a pasha weep.

WHAT TO EXPECT

The true tastes of the Middle East remain hidden firmly behind family doors. Fortunately, instead of having to throw yourself onto some unsuspecting family in downtown Amman, you can invite yourself to feast at Beit Sitti's dining table, on meals you've learnt to cook from scratch.

Before you put on your pinafore, you'll be given some insight into the

Wrangle yourself an invitation across the threshold of a typical Jordanian home, and you'll find you've fallen into a culinary wonderland.

importance of mealtimes in the Middle East. In Jordan it really is all about the food. Gathering together for a meal plays a pivotal role in the preservation of culture, and skilled home cooks are celebrated here. And no wonder. Levantine cuisine is never going to be your whip-it-up-in-five-minutes, bing-bang-bosh fare. At the bare basics there's a lot of finicky chopping and mixing to contend with.

Making a proper *muttabel* (spicy eggplant dip) requires eggplants char-grilled to creamy-smoky precision. *Fattet jaj* (a layered peasant-dish of toasted pita, meat and yoghurt) requires a garlic-tahini-yoghurt blend that is punchy yet not overpowering. You'll learn to perfect the delicate pairings of flavour and spice, and find out why short cuts simply don't cut the sumac.

All that sweating over a hot stove pays off in the end results. On Beit Sitti's balcony, you'll feast on your menu of Levantine finery while the hubbub of modern Amman plays out below.

Experiencing culture through cuisine starts with an adventure in Amman's market.

BELLY UP FOR DANCE
CLASSES IN ISTANBUL

Duration Two hours ✳ **Cost** Around €100 per class ✳ **Outcome** A curvier waistline, enhanced fitness and a dash of Ottoman panache ✳ **Where** Les Arts Turcs, Istanbul, Turkey

As a belly dancer you get to indulge your sensual side while strengthening your core like a triathlete.

Put a shimmy in your step and take belly-dancing lessons in Istanbul, where the Ottoman arts have flourished for centuries.

WHAT TO EXPECT

Wandering around Istanbul can be almost like sliding through the layers of an archaeological dig: this is a city that wears its history on its sleeve. One moment you're inhabiting the dynamic present as you graze on mod-Turkish meze in the upbeat bars of Beyoğlu; the next you're strolling over the Ancient Roman site of the Hippodrome, which hosted chariot races in AD 203, to check out a column originally erected at Delphi to celebrate the Greeks' victory over the Persians.

And it's not only the landscape that takes you back. Istanbul's cultural traditions are still thoroughly kicking in the modern city. Taking tea in a tulip glass, puffing on a water pipe, soaking in a 16th-century bath house – they're all a pleasant form of time travel.

If you're looking for a more active engagement with the past, belly-dancing lessons could be just the ticket. Turkish belly dancers have been shaking it for centuries. More energetic and playful than the Middle Eastern forms, Turkish belly dance also makes use of *zils* (finger-cymbals).

All in all, learning to shake your belly is a great way to get fit, express yourself, tone up your muscles and ring your bells.

How it suits you

Artistic types will be in heaven – this is a dance form with lots of room for creative expression. Once you've learnt the basic moves, the way you twist it is up to you. Historical buffs will enjoy musing on the many generations of dancers who shimmy behind them, and where and how they wiggled. You rational types may find the dance beneficial – the belly is said by many cultures to be the seat of feeling, so getting in touch with it could provide a pleasant leaven to your logical life.

What you'll get from it

★ **Going in circles** Turkish culture has a lot of sinuosity. The calligraphy, the Whirling Dervishes, the arabesques in its design – they're all built on the curve. Belly dancing puts you right inside that infinity sign.

★ **A little of the lithe** Belly dancing is great for your cardio fitness, your coordination, your muscle tone and your waistline.

★ **Permission to shine** Istanbul's bazaars abound with outrageously opulent belly-dancing costumes, all glitter and colour and mirrors. Of course, it'd just be silly to buy one – unless you know the moves, that is, and then you've got every reason to buy six.

Practical details

Les Arts Turcs (lesartsturcs.com) in Istanbul gives private belly-dancing classes, so you can learn to roll without feeling self-conscious. The school can also arrange group lessons.

Other options

Put a different spin on your belly-shake by trying out classes in the Middle East. In some Arabic countries there is a stigma attached to belly dancing, but in more liberal countries there is an abundance of choice. Check out the worldwide **Belly Dance Classes** (bellydanceclasses.net) directory for classes in Israel and the UAE.

Doing it at home

Belly dancing has become an increasingly popular pastime in the West, and classes are easy to find. Just Google your home town to find a directory. Many belly-dancing schools give performances on stage or as part of festivals. If you've ever longed to don sequins and finger-cymbals in the public arena, this is your moment. Go on, make the Ottomans proud!

DISTIL A DREAM DRAM IN SCOTLAND

Duration Five days ✻ **Cost** £1000 ✻ **Outcome** Learn the ropes of illicit whisky-making and make off with a cask of the finished product ✻ **Where** Aultbea, northwest Scotland

How it suits you

The course gives wannabe bootleggers the run of the distillery (and its two stills), so small groups (one to four) are best, with two people (one per still) being ideal. It's a bonding experience (you're there together mixing barley in the middle of nowhere for hours), so go for quality time away with someone you care about, who doesn't mind isolation and who has sticking power (half-finished whisky tastes disgusting).

What you'll get from it

★ **A cask of whisky** You can smuggle away the fruits of your labours: a 5-litre cask of moonshine (UK tax and duty prepaid).

★ **Whisky history** It's not just the distilling ... you'll get a vivid impression of what the world of 18th-century whisky-making was like, discovering how the whole community (local landowners included) got involved.

★ **Local sightseeing** See the caves and tunnels where smugglers once stashed supplies.

★ **Whisky-tasting** Whisky-making isn't all hard work at the Drumchork. Come evening, you can whisky-taste at a bar stocked with over 700 other whiskies (one of the world's best selections) and sample the palate match, where staff will recommend the perfect dram to counter-balance your dinner. You'll find a smoky Old Pulteney single-malt goes down wonderfully with some of Loch Ewe's famous smoked salmon.

Practical details

Drumchork Lodge Hotel (hotelaultbea.co.uk) and **Loch Ewe Distillery** (lochewedistillery.co.uk) are 112km northwest of Inverness. Whisky-making courses are available year-round.

Other options

Bladnoch Distillery (bladnoch.co.uk) in Bladnoch, Scotland, runs three-day courses in all aspects of whisky production. The **Beverage Academy** (beverageacademy.com) in San Francisco hosts classes in everything from bourbon- to tequila-making.

Doing it at home

You might want to avoid unlicensed distilling on your own patch, but you can 'take spirits into your own hands' by arranging a home whisky-tasting. Buy whiskies from various regions of the world and make notes on taste and appearance with friends.

WHAT TO EXPECT

Fling caution to the wind and sign up for Scotland's only illicit whisky-making course. In an age where big distilleries remotely control much of their whisky-making by computer, you'll be starting the fire to heat your water and stirring in barley with a spurtle.

Up on lonely Loch Ewe, with mountains on one side and the fierce Atlantic on the other, the setting of this old Highland lodge

Create whisky, the water of life, as it was originally done – in a back room high in Scotland's hills, dodging the eyes of the law – and get away with your own stash of spirit, too.

alone evokes century-old images of Scots battling the elements and the law to eke out a living – and today's whisky industry is of course the result of them winning that battle. Times were traditionally tough, especially so for whisky-makers, who struggled to produce the liquor under the ever-watchful eyes of the excise men, and undertook treacherous journeys to sell the precious liquor.

The folk at Drumchork Lodge Hotel poignantly re-create every part of the ancient art of whisky-making, from barley-soaking and fermentation to maturation in old sherry barrels. Budding distillers get a crash course in how the spirit was concocted before the 1823 Excise Act made whisky production legal. Five days and two distillations later, you'll be taking home your own cask

of freshly made liquor.

You'll have defied the law to do so, too – whisky at the on-site Loch Ewe Distillery is distilled in 120-litre stills: a whopping 1680 litres below the legal limit for a Scotch whisky still. This does mean what you'll make can't officially be called whisky – instead you can call it *uisge beatha*, Gaelic for 'water of life' – but it will taste just as good.

Holy spirit: the angels take their share of maturing whisky as it evaporates through the barrel.

Inside Islam: take the opportunity to understand the world's second-largest religion.

LEARN ABOUT ISLAM
IN ISTANBUL

Duration 10 days ✳ **Cost** €745 ✳ **Outcome** Deeper understanding, greater tolerance and a brush with the divine ✳ **Where** Istanbul and Konya, Turkey

Dawn in Istanbul is a marvellous cacophony of voices, as the call to prayer issues from countless minarets. Many Western visitors pull the blankets over their heads – but you, as a foreigner immersing yourself in Muslim practices and in tune with the waking city, will be up and out of bed to join the rhythm of prayer.

As a 'Muslim for a month', you'll find out why dervishes spin and what *sahleb* is made of. You'll learn the basics of prayer and devotional singing, see an Islamic wedding ceremony, and visit Istanbul's most spectacular mosques. You'll deepen your knowledge of the Quran and of Sufisim, the mystical side of Islam. You'll study the teachings of Rumi and visit his birthplace. (You'll also give up pork and alcohol for the duration – but you are allowed to smoke!)

Experiencing Istanbul from the perspective of the religion that drives the city will make all your encounters here more profound, and give you an unparalleled insight into Turkey's culture. Think of it like an 'access all areas' pass – instead of just watching from the audience, you'll be standing in the wings and having deep-and-meaningfuls in the band room.

How it suits you

Naturally, spiritual types will eat up this opportunity to experience a new relationship to the divine, especially when focused through the hypnotic prism of Sufism. Social butterflies will pick up a host of new talking points for conversations with the locals, and organised types will get their teeth into the five-times-a-day discipline of prayer. Altruistic peeps will love the charitable side of Islam.

What you'll get from it

★ **Journey into your inner life** Rumi urges us to 'search the secret jewel in the mountain of your body'. This is your chance to do a little spiritual spelunking.
★ **An informed view** In non-Islamic countries, particularly after the events of 9/11, misconceptions and bigotries about Muslims abound. Your experience will help you make up your own mind about one of the world's most prevalent religions.
★ **Interaction** Istanbul is a predominantly Muslim city – and a very welcoming one. Your attempts to participate in the city's customs will be greeted warmly.

Practical details

The **Muslim for a Month** (muslimforamonth.com) program is run by World Weavers, an NGO devoted to 'promoting positive cultural experiences'. Check out at a detailed itinerary online (the 'for a month' is poetic licence, as courses run for 10 days).

Other options

You can also try out the Buddhist lifestyle by being a **Monk for a Month** (monkforamonth.com), a program run by World Weavers in Thailand and Tibet.

Doing it at home

Islam might not be well understood in the West, but there's definitely an attraction to Sufisim and, in particular, Rumi. Studies in Sufisim in your city may be a Google search away; if not, you can easily lay your hands on a translation of Rumi's beautiful mystic poetry.

Discover the daily realities of one of the world's most misunderstood religions in Turkey's progressive capital.

BECOME TOP DOG IN THE YUKON

Duration Three to 10 days ✴ **Cost** From C$950 ✴ **Outcome** Gain insights into dog training and retrace the route of the fabled Yukon Quest dogsled race ✴ **Where** Yukon Territory, Canada

How it suits you

This is definitely one for the intrepid adventurer – it takes a daring spirit to want to mush through winter just shy of the Arctic Circle. If you're camping out, you'll experience life on the snow at something like -20°C or -30°C. For the chiefs among you, although it won't feel like it sometimes, you're the one in charge – those dogs out front are under your control, and at times it's almost regal, being towed through a fairy-tale landscape as you stand tall at the back of the pack.

What you'll get from it

★ **Space to reflect** The spruce and poplar forests of the Yukon are vast, empty places. Once the dogs have their line (see Precision, below), there's little for the mind to do but ponder.

★ **Humility** The moose tracks in the snow, the dogs asleep on the ice, the dancing Northern Lights – it's difficult to feel like the centre of the universe out here.

★ **Precision** There's no near-enough-is-good-enough on a sled; get your weight distribution wrong into a corner, or brake too hard, and you might end up attached to a tree rather than your dog team.

Practical details

Most dogsledding operations are based out of Whitehorse, the Yukon's capital city. Trips usually operate between about January and April. Two of the most experienced operators are **Cathers Wilderness Adventures** (cathersadventures. com) and **Muktuk Adventures** (muktuk.com).

Other options

In Greenland, ride a dog team across one of the iciest lands of all. If you're in Finland, emulate Santa on a reindeer safari, or see how the pros do it in Alaska by witnessing the **Iditarod** (iditarod.com) dogsled race in March.

Doing it at home

Train up your own team of Alaskan huskies – or your family pooch. Even in countries without much snow, there are often races or events using scooters or rigs instead of snow sleds.

WHAT TO EXPECT

Dogsledding, also known as mushing, looks simple – after all, the dogs do all the work, right? Wrong. Mushing isn't as straightforward as stepping up and gliding away through the spruce forest. And you can forget dog training – it's the dogs that will be training you!

Learning the art of dogsledding begins with theory. You'll be talked through the skills – braking, keeping a tight line,

Head to the Yukon, dogsledding's spiritual home, to learn the finer points of mushing, leading a team of Alaskan huskies across a snow-covered landscape.

steering by weight shifts, hanging onto the sled even when you fall off – and then it's out onto the snow.

You'll begin with just a handful of dogs, moving up to more powerful teams as you become more proficient. Through the forest you'll practise your newly acquired skills, gauging your performance by the response of your dogs. If they're peeping over their shoulders at you as they run, you're still earning their confidence. If they're running ahead without looking back at you, you know you're in control.

As part of your instruction, you'll probably end up camping out at least one night in the forest. Even as you wonder whether your nose really has petrified in the subzero conditions, it's your job to make sure the dogs get their breakfast before you do.

Longer sledding trips may follow sections of the Yukon Quest, the event that has immortalised the Yukon as the dogsledding heartland. The so-called 'toughest dogsled race on the planet' covers 1600km between Whitehorse and Fairbanks, Alaska – it's a fair boast to say you've led your own dog team along even part of the route.

Learn fa'a Samoa, the Samoan way, at a traditional kava ceremony.

SOAK UP THE TRADITION
OF *KAVA* IN SAMOA

Duration Six hours ✻ **Cost** US$60 ✻ **Outcome** Anthropology 101 with a close-up look at daily life in a traditional Samoan village ✻ **Where** Sa'anapu village, Upolu island, Samoa

Seated cross-legged on a mat, eyeballed by a bare-chested, *lavalava*-clad man displaying his magnificent *pe'a* (full-body tattoo), you are quickly drawn into a different world. Fa'atupu, your village-born *matai* (chief) host and guide, will patiently teach you what you need to know when it comes to the world of *kava*, from the significance of the *fale* setting to all the *kava* protocols – where people sit, the roles they play, the speeches they make, the mixing of the *kava* and its ceremonial ingestion.

Samoa's traditions and culture – its fabled Fa'a Samoa (Samoan way) – have evolved over 3000 years into a body of wisdom based on healthy interdependence with the coastal rainforests, coral reefs and spirit world. One of the most ancient *Fa'a* traditions is the legendary commemorative *kava* ceremony (called *'ava* in Samoa), an education which serves as your welcome to Sa'anapu village.

You'll learn how the *kava* ceremony is rooted in royal lore, and is a powerful forum for expressions of peace and respect between leaders, an authoritative council setting for making decisions about land and people.

By the time you get to drink the *kava* – an acquired taste aided by the numbing of your tongue, lips and mouth – you can identify the *taupou* (virgin princess) by her fine robe and feathered head gear. You know how to receive the libation and what is expected of you. You have, in essence, become part of the village, so that you can then share in its day-to-day life and meet its people.

This you then do on a guided walking tour of the village. While tipsily wandering, you'll see how the locals live on and use the land, including the adjacent Sa'anapu forest and Sataoa Mangrove Conservation Area, the largest mangrove system in Samoa.

How it suits you

An initiation into Fa'a Samoa is suited to people with deep respect for spirituality and tradition, who appreciate the privilege of being invited to participate in a kava ceremony. Once welcomed into the community, even if only for a day, don't be shy – a people-person will discover many new friends.

What you'll get from it

★ **Cultural insight** The *kava* ceremony is the ultimate introduction to Samoan culture – you *live* tradition rather than just observe it.

★ **Nature appreciation** Samoans' use of indigenous plants, especially the coconut, pepper (aka *kava*) and Intsia trees (or merbau), is an integral part of their everyday alimentary, ritual and artistic lives.

★ **Community connection** This may be the closest a visitor can get to experiencing traditional village life in and meeting the people of Samoa.

Practical details

Made possible by **Samoa Urban Adventures** (urbanadventures.com, click on Samoa), this experience can be booked in both the wet and dry seasons.

Other options

Although sometimes known by different names, *kava* is part of religious and cultural traditions throughout western Oceania, including Fiji, Tonga and Vanuatu. Sharing *kava* with locals, in their countries and abroad, is almost always by invitation only.

Doing it at home

As an honorary *matai* and ambassador of Samoan culture, bring Fa'a Samoa to your friends and family by staging your own kava ceremony. Seat everyone, explain their roles and responsibilities, and the nature of the objects they hold. Establish your village.

Visit a village of ancient origin to learn the intricacies of the venerable *kava* ceremony, held in a stunning *fale* (traditional house).

RUN LIKE THE WIND IN THE RIFT VALLEY

Duration Two weeks ❋ **Cost** £899 ❋ **Outcome** Speed, strength, stamina – basically, a faster, fitter you, and one that's inspired to get even better ❋ **Where** Iten, western Kenya

How it suits you

There's more to this than shaving some seconds off your 10km personal best: living in a Kenyan village for a fortnight, running its dusty tracks and meeting its people, is more eye-opening than trying to cover the whole country. Even so, this trip is for the intrepid adventurer and the active do-er – someone who wants to achieve, not watch. And the anal-retentive fitness freak will love poring over those detailed training plans, and calculating just how to run that little bit faster.

What you'll get from it

★ **Fitness** Early-morning runs, training at altitude, fartleking (alternating fast and slow), hill repeats, core conditioning in the gym. This is a bootcamp, not a break – albeit a bootcamp with safari side trips – but you'll feel all the better for it.
★ **Speed** Fitter, yes, and faster too: running alongside local Olympians should whittle down your PBs, and teach you to run the 'Kenyan way'. Well, they seem to be on to something ...
★ **Personal achievement** Your muscles will strengthen, your legs tone and your mind clear – you'll feel like a champion.
★ **Humility** With all your financial advantages and fancy trappings, you can't hold a candle to these super-driven athletes.

Practical details

Kenya Experience (traininkenya.com) offers scheduled two-week training camps, including guided runs, coached workshops, training talks and tips on doing it the 'Kenyan way'. Excursions, including a safari to Lake Nakuru, are also available.

Other options

Take to the Welsh fells for off-road running lessons in rugged Snowdonia, or delve into Mexico's Copper Canyons to run with the super-humanly speedy Tarahumara Indians. Or book a stay at **Club La Santa** (clublasanta.com), a sport-focused resort in the Canary Islands that hosts famous athletes and runs a range of training camps.

Doing it at home

Simple: just keep running. It's easy to slip this most basic form of exercise into your daily routine: it can be done anytime, anywhere by anyone; it's cheap too. Trot to work, jog at lunchtime – and use motivation gleaned in Kenya to power the rest of your life.

WHAT TO EXPECT

You can expect hard graft, that's what. But then, you don't sign up for two weeks' training at Iten High Altitude Camp if you want to laze by a pool. This village on the Great Rift Valley Escarpment, teetering up at 2400 metres, is certainly scenic but not obviously remarkable. That is, until you find out that it's home to perhaps the greatest concentration of elite long-

On your marks, get set and go to Kenya, where one tiny village – home to some of the world's best runners – can really put a spring in your step.

distance athletes in the world.

Be it elevation, lifestyle, diet, ethos – some auspicious collision of cosmic forces has occurred around this humble hub, making it ridiculously good at producing runners. And now regular jogging Joes and Joannas can join in.

Stay at Iten's plush training camp and you'll be put through your literal paces. There are predawn alarm calls for early leg stretches – it's best to hit the dirt tracks before the equatorial heat builds, plus sunrises here are spectacular motivators. There are punishing hills that will make you weep, then core-stability drills that will make you weep more. And then there are speed sessions that will have you eating the dust of your unmatchable Kenyan co-runners as soon as the whistle goes.

You'll dash past mud huts and overladen donkeys, listen to lectures from past Olympians and watch in awe as the local stars do their sprints round the Kameriny Track. In short, you'll learn to run like a Kenyan – even if you can't quite manage to keep up.

Experience, stride by stride, the training ethos that has made the Kenyans a formidable force in world athletics.

FIND FOOD AT YOUR
FEET IN SAN FRAN

Duration Two hours ✳ **Cost** US$30 ✳ **Outcome** Taste new flavours, discover nature's bounty and get tips on how to survive post-apocalypse ✳ **Where** San Francisco, California, US

You'll never look at a leafy suburb in quite the same way again.

> **Get a taste of San Francisco's urban foraging renaissance on an edible tour of the city's parks, gardens and sidewalks – it's a grass roots glimpse of a food revolution.**

WHAT TO EXPECT

Scrounging for food – isn't that considered uncouth? Not in San Francisco, where even the most exclusive restaurants add foraged lettuces, wildflowers and seaweed to their dishes.

It might be the combination of lush landscapes and freethinking culture, but the world's biggest food trends, from the organic food movement to the mixed greens salad, have their roots here in San Francisco. For a taste of one of the latest food trends, join Forage SF's Wild Food Walks and head on and off path through local parks in search of edible plants.

You'll be surprised how often your guide will stop to point out what's edible as you forage, gather, glean, scavenge, wildcraft, scrump – whatever word you want to use to describe the age-old practice of finding something to eat wherever you happen to be.

The stinging nettles lining the trail are way more nutritious than kale, and those pine branches overhead can be brewed up into a cold-busting tea. And if you can smell licorice in the air, it'll be the aniseed-flavoured pollen of wild fennel wafting in the breeze like yellow pixie dust.

The plant varieties might differ in your hometown, but you'll still pick up useful tips on how to spot healthy plants and how to harvest them sustainably, ensuring the outdoor larder is always stocked for the next forager.

How it suits you

Foraging involves stomping through tall brush, breaking open prickly seeds and flipping over rocks, so intrepid travellers will be in their element. Since where and how much you find varies depending on the season, you'll need to tap into your spontaneous side and go with the flow. You'll feed your inner hermit when you brush off the dirt and bugs and take your first bite.

What you'll get from it

★ **Chef know-how** Cooks around the world are crazy for foraging. Next time you taste a tangy yellow flower garnishing your plate, you'll know what it is (oxalis, also known as wood sorrel).

★ **Survival** You'll tune into your hunter-gatherer instincts when you rediscover why red holly berries are deceptively festive.

★ **Tranquillity** You'll have the opportunity to check out some of San Francisco's prettiest green spaces during the walk.

Practical details

Walks organised by **Forage SF** (foragesf.com) take place most Saturdays year-round. The lushest months for edible plants are February through April. Seasonal mushroom walks are held December through January. Forage SF also offers custom tours – just be sure to wear a pair of sturdy walking shoes or boots, especially in wet weather – or join Forage SF's monthly dinners ($85 to $100) for eight courses of entirely foraged, local ingredients including wild boar, snails and albacore (a type of tuna).

Other options

In New York, **Steve 'Wildman' Brill** (wildmanstevebrill.com), who was once arrested for eating a dandelion in Central Park, has been leading tours in the park and other urban areas, with the approval of the Park Service. And for the ultimate taste of fine dining meets foraging, make a reservation at **Coi** (coirestaurant.com) in San Francisco, **Noma** (noma.dk) in Copenhagen or **Attica** (attica.com.au) in Melbourne.

Doing it at home

Check online or at your library for resources on your local plants (and foraging laws). Take care with mushrooms, which are tricky to identify and best left to the professionals. If you have a spare corner of your backyard or a window box, let nature take its course. In a few months, you could easily have enough greens to spice up a meal.

STRIKE A POSE, DANCING BALINESE STYLE

Duration From one hour ✳ **Cost** 75,000 rupiah per hour ✳ **Outcome** New-found grace, Balinese cultural insights and a fondness for gamelan ✳ **Where** Ubud, Bali, Indonesia

WHAT TO EXPECT

The village of Ubud has always been a hotbed of fine and applied Balinese arts. For creative types, there's a little bit of everything on offer here – sculpture, woodcarving, mask-making, jewellery-making, painting, shadow puppetry, gamelan-playing and, a perennial favourite, dancing.

Dance is central to Balinese culture, as it is in any place where Hinduism is the majority religion. Several of its most dominant traditional forms, like *barong, legong* and *kecak*, are now internationally renowned. A distinguishing feature of all Balinese dance forms is a mesmerising complexity of coded movements of the eyes, face, hands, arms, body and feet. The devil (in this case, Rangda, a mythical witch representing evil) really is in the detail.

The Pondok Pekak Library & Learning Center is a modest community hub – Ubud's only library – that provides one-on-one and group lessons in the Indonesian language and the 'Art of Bali' to anyone beguiled by Balinese culture.

In its peaceful central performance space, you stand before a guru (men only with a man, women with a woman) who patiently leads you through choreographed exercises of increasing complexity and beauty. As you learn each step, one at a time, you'll start to see the dancer's intricate body articulations with different eyes as your body adjusts to the unique gestural complexity of Balinese dance.

How it suits you

Learning any kind of cultural dance takes patience, practice and a belief in one's inner Fred or Ginger. Given the intricacies of *barong, legong* and *kecak,* you should have a strong artistic temperament that includes poise and a good sense of rhythm. Attention to detail is also critical – you have to know what part of the body to move, and precisely when and how to do it.

What you'll get from it

★ **Cultural insights** Balinese dance is a gateway to Balinese culture, inextricably intertwined with its music and ritual.
★ **Community connection** Directly through the music and dance, but also via time spent at the library in its reading rooms and during family-friendly workshops and performances, you'll meet locals committed to their culture.
★ **Responsible spending** The library generates most of its operating funds, especially free educational services to the local community, through these workshops and programs.

Practical details

The **Pondok Pekak Library & Learning Center** is adjacent to the football field in the heart of Ubud. Classes are best arranged in person with library staff, usually with 24 or 48 hours' notice. Major arts institutions like the **Agung Rai Museum of Art** (ARMA; armabali.com) and the **Museum Puri Lukisan** mpl-ubud.com) are geared more for group workshops rather than one-on-one classes.

Other options

Unfortunately, Balinese dance classes and workshops held outside of Indonesia are not very common. Exceptional operations do exist, including **Dharma Swara** (dharmaswara.org) and **BALAM** (balamdance.org) in the US, and **Balinesedance** (balinesedance.org) in the UK. Contact your nearest Indonesian consulate for more local options.

Doing it at home

One of the virtues of dance is that it can be performed anywhere. With friends and family, you can demonstrate the specific Balinese movements of just one body part or put a series of movements together. Be sure to secure some gamelan music so you can stay rhythmically and culturally in sync.

Wrapped in your sarong, you strike a pose. Then another and another, each posture a slight variation of the one before. String them together and you'll discover the cultural weave that binds Balinese art together ... and you to it.

The subtle, complex moves that characterise Balinese dance are sure to keep you intrigued.

BUILD A HOME SWEET SNOWHOME IN CANADA

Duration One day ✳ **Cost** C$150 ✳ **Outcome** Igloo-building skills, rugged charm and new respect for Inuit skills ✳ **WHERE** Coast Mountains, British Columbia, Canada

Carve out a snow shelter that's up to 50°C snugger inside than the chilly outside temperature, and gain a potentially life-saving skill in Inuit territory.

WHAT TO EXPECT

You're stuck in a freezing blizzard on a bleak mountain. But everything you need to make your own shelter is around you, provided you have the essential snow saw and shovel, that is – note to self: must always carry a snow saw and shovel. Igloo construction takes time, so don't expect to get toasty immediately. First, there's a lot of stomping about in your boots to compact the snow enough to make solid blocks. Then waiting an hour for the snow to set before carving them out. So take the chance to admire the sturdy pine trees around you.

The most surprising thing about piecing together the igloo is that when you place the blocks at an angle, they don't topple over. The igloo sits together like a 3D jigsaw puzzle, spiralling inwards till there is only the roof of the dome to cap off.

It's hard to imagine how warm it can be inside the igloo while bitter winds howl outside. The secret to the Inuit construction is the entrance tunnel, which traps the settling cold air, while you sleep on the raised sleeping area with the rising warm air. You end up with a soundproof igloo that, if properly made, can take the weight of a person standing on the roof, despite being made out of snow – yes, that soft stuff that melts. The igloo you built in three hours will last all winter and endure hurricane-strength winds.

How it suits you

For the intrepid traveller, this may be your idea of paradise, a picturesque world of snow-laden trees and pristine spaces. You will feel satisfied knowing you have the ability to make a shelter from any desolate snowy landscape, with no other human footprints in sight. This is quite literally a team-building exercise, so leaders will relish bringing a team of travellers together to build an igloo. Flat-pack furniture may have become child's play for DIY-types now: your next challenge is to make a home with two tools and just one part – snow.

What you'll get from it

★ **Confidence** Knowing you can survive a snowy wilderness will make you feel self-assured and independent.
★ **Stamina** Grit your teeth and ignore your shivering body, because once your igloo is built you'll get a warm glow.
★ **Peace** The silence inside an igloo will make you feel far from civilisation and close to nature. The sunlight shining through the igloo's snow blocks is nature's own cathedral windows.
★ **A feeling for snow** Being in these vast empty spaces of Canada will give you insight into what it must have been like to live off the land as an Inuk before modern society influenced new generations of Inuit to move away from building igloos (except for hunting trips).

Practical details

Westcoast Adventures (westcoast-adventures.com) runs overnight adventures where you sleep in your own igloo.

Other options

Nature Travels (naturetravels.co.uk) offers a four-day course in Swedish Lapland, sleeping in your own igloo. Check the **CSIRO** (csiro.au, search 'igloo') website, and make your own model igloo at home from ice cubes.

Doing it at home

Now that you know how to construct an igloo, try building one on your next ski trip to show off après-ski. Inuit once built grand igloos with multiple rooms. Create one with friends, then compare your handiwork by renting a ready-made igloo in the Swiss Alps large enough for parties.

There's no central heating but this skill could save your life in a snowy wilderness.

FOLLOW THE FOOTSTEPS
OF PYGMIES IN UGANDA

Duration Five hours ✳ **Cost** US$70 ✳ **Outcome** Learn survival skills, have an immersive jungle experience and meet African pygmy elders ✳ **Where** Next to Bwindi Impenetrable Forest, Uganda

You'll get the warmest of welcomes as the Batwa people invite you to experience their forest.

With tribal elders as your guides, travel back 1000 years to when the Batwa pygmies thrived, and learn the jungle skills of lighting a fire with sticks and using a bow and arrow.

WHAT TO EXPECT

They say the city's a jungle, but out here you really need bush skills to survive. Medicinal plants, animal traps, bush honey and fire sticks – spend a day in the jungle with the Batwa pygmies and you'll experience a threatened way of life in one of Africa's few living history museums.

Indigenous to Uganda and Rwanda, the Batwa are perhaps the largest and longest-surviving pygmy tribe in the world. And yet their ancient way of life is seriously under threat. Forest nomads for thousands of years, the Batwa were evicted in 1992 from part of their ancestral homeland in southwest Uganda to make way for Bwindi Impenetrable Forest, a protected conservation area for endangered mountain gorillas.

Despite this setback, the Batwa are working to preserve their ancient lifestyle and perpetuate their precious traditions. This unique Batwa Experience is a partial fulfilment of that dream. On 40 hectares of old-growth forest abutting the off-limits parkland, the Batwa have re-created to the fullest extent possible their cultural heritage in their native ancestral environment, and with the full involvement of the community.

With Batwa pygmies to guide you, you'll take a 45-minute jungle hike to a remote mountain-top *banda* (hut), and hear Batwa folklore directly from the mouths of elders. Join in Batwa song and dance, harvest honey, visit dwellings and shrines, inspect animal traps, discover medicinal plants, weave baskets ... and at the climax of this deeply immersive cultural plunge, join a mock hunting party and try your hand at making fire using sticks and shooting a traditional Batwa bow and arrow. Jungle tasks such as these have kept the Batwa alive in the African rainforest for millennia.

How it suits you

The Batwa Experience is an active, hands-on learning day trip that favours the adventurous. You'll enjoy it if you're not shy, and unabashed about taking your turn at things that may be unfamiliar to you – and that you're pretty much guaranteed not to get right the first time you try.

What you'll get from it

★ **Bush skills** Who can tell when knowing how to use a bushman's bow and arrow will come in handy?

★ **Cultural insights** Even though it's a staged demonstration, the experience is as accurate a portrayal as exists of what Batwa life was like in the forest.

★ **Community connection** In Uganda, only the Batwa Experience has guides who actually lived the primeval culture they're sharing.

Practical details

Book the **Batwa Experience** (www.batwaexperience.com) online, directly from the Batwa Development Program. Be prepared for a challenging but not overly strenuous hike; wear long pants, proper hiking shoes and a hat. Bring rain gear and sunscreen too.

Other options

In Australia, several community-based groups offer single- and multiday Aboriginal cultural immersion packages. Or go **Picnic with the Penan** (picnicwiththepenan.org), and spend a week with the indigenous Penan people of Borneo.

Doing it at home

Find local equivalents of the Bwindi forest wood species needed for starting a fire and stringing a bow. The rest is all practice, practice, practice – something best enjoyed when you challenge your friends to light your barbecue with only a couple of sticks (that aren't matches).

CAST A FISHING NET
IN SOUTHERN BRAZIL

Duration Four hours ✳ **Cost** R$260 ✳ **Outcome** Traditional fishing skills, Old Man of the Sea lore and a sea cruise with a difference ✳ **Where** Pântano do Sul, Florianopolis, Brazil

How it suits you

If you're spontaneous, ready to jump into action but also happy to sit back and observe, this experience will suit you down to the ground. Although the local fishermen follow a set routine, the ocean is a fickle partner and you must be prepared to, well, go with the flow. A solid pair of sea legs helps a lot, too.

What you'll get from it

★ **Cultural insight** By participating in the fishermen's daily routine, with explanations from an expert local guide, you'll live the essence of this endangered Brazilian coastal culture.
★ **Nature appreciation** This trip treats you to some of the region's best-preserved and most beautiful out-of-the-way locations.
★ **Tall tales** Pântano do Sul is the most important and traditional of Florianopolis' fishing villages, where lifelong mariners tell amazing stories of past exploits over lunch.

Practical details

The Estrelas do Mar experience can be arranged through **Brazil Trails** (braziltrails.com, click on 'Tourism Experiences' and 'Fishermen Life'), which also offers an in-depth seven-day version. All activities are subject to sea conditions and weather.

Other options

The Costa Rican community of Tárcoles in Puntarenas offers similar fishing trips, a cooperative fisheries warehouse tour and mollusc-gathering activities through **Consorcio Por La Mar** (consorcioporlamar.com). In Florida, contemporary fishing practices may be far from traditional, but spear fishing is an ancient method that's made Key West famous.

Doing it at home

While you may be hard pressed to find a use for enclosure fishery nets near home, your new understanding of threatened traditional fishing practices can be turned to good effect. Learn about local traditions so you can decide if you want to buy local and natural.

WHAT TO EXPECT

Florianopolis is called the 'Island of Magic' for good reason: its mix of nature, culture and coastal ease is addictive. Considered by many to be Brazil's surf capital, Florianopolis has also been described as the hippest year-round beach scene in South America.

But, of course, it wasn't always this way. Not so long ago, the community's

Spend a morning with sure-oared local fishermen, and gain an understanding of the waves, tides and people of Brazil's Island of Magic.

economic engines were fishing and agriculture. While commerce and services now dominate, traditional fishing operations still exist and, in a bid to preserve their ancient way of life, some villages have resisted the lure of modernity.

Under the guidance of the Instituto Ilhas do Brasil, the beach village of Pântano do Sul has established an award-winning community-based initiative called Estrelas do Mar (Stars of the Sea). Its aim: to pair up-for-anything travellers with local fishermen in a hands-on morning on the water.

While you shadow the actions of your caretakers in a typical fisherman's boat, your mission is to learn the practices of traditional fishing, including inspecting, casting and collecting *pescaria de cerco* (enclosure fishery) nets; sorting fish; and reading the tides, the weather and the sea conditions.

And don't worry, it's not all work: a swim break and typical local lunch are included.

Learn to cast your net along the region's breathtaking beaches.

FIND YOUR GROOVE IN GHANA

Duration Four weeks ✳ **Cost** A$3800 ✳ **Outcome** The ability to drum like a full-blooded African musician, a new sense of rhythm and loss of inhibitions ✳ **Where** Nungua village, Ghana

Follow the beat of Ghana's masters of percussion.

Get to grips with African percussion, dance and song in Ghana, an exotic locale for a month of intensive musical training.

Gershwin might not have been thinking about African drumming and dancing when he wrote 'I got rhythm, I got music ... Who could ask for anything more?' but it most certainly applies to Nii Tettey Tetteh, the Ghanaian musician and composer who started the Ghana Drum School. The village of Nungua, 15km from the Ghana capital Accra, is the setting for four weeks of African drum and dance and song.

This isn't some namby-pamby 'cultural' tour with a token music segment. You'll be attending daily four-hour lessons on drumming and dancing, taught by the staff of 10. Lessons revolve around the *djembe* and *kpanlogo* drums, a *shekere* (gourd shaker) and a bell. You'll be taught a diverse range of African musical styles, and while drumming is the core of the course, singing and dancing are an integral part of the experience.

The school believes in the practical application of skills: whether you're a rank beginner or someone who's had experience in percussions, live group performances are part of the whole deal. Don't fret; stage fright is surprisingly easy to overcome because the African *joie de vivre* is really quite infectious.

Instruction goes beyond the classroom, too. Outside of official lessons, you'll head out on field trips and be taken to watch performances by local musical groups.

How it suits you

For the cultural traveller, well, this is the real deal. You'll be instructed in the heart of Ghana, by bona fide musicians and dancers. Heck, even all three daily meals will be Ghanaian (sorry, no hamburgers and chips here). And if music stirs your soul, your drumming will form the soundtrack for the friendships you'll be forging with your instructors and fellow course mates across the four weeks. For the rock star, you'll be performing several times in front of local audiences. There's no better testing ground to prove your musical mettle.

What you'll get from it

★ **Culture** It's not just about learning the music and dance moves, it's also about immersing yourself in the unique spirit that drives this brand of African culture. Ghana's music is steeped in traditional rituals, something you will witness and be a part of.
★ **Fitness** Drumming and dancing will work up a sweat. Four hours a day might not sound like much but it can get intense.
★ **Rhythm** It's not just about being able to play an instrument, but also about getting into the heart and soul of it. The cheerful, uplifting spirit of African drumming will make you tap your toes and shake your body – all the while drumming, too.

Practical details

Sign up for the four-week **Kusun Study Tour** (ghanadrumschool. com) via Jane Pentland in Australia. The fee includes full board and lodging, plus an extra A$180 if you'd like to purchase your own drum equipment.

Other options

There are heaps of African drumming schools around the world. Check out **African Drumming** (africandrumming.com.au) in Melbourne, **Drum Africa** (drumafrica.co.uk) in London or **Wula Drum** (wuladrum.com) in New York. Brazilian drumming also offers a similar style and spirit – look for courses run by local clubs.

Doing it at home

Join a local African band or have a mash-up with Brazilian drummers. Or offer your hot drumming skills to any band that wants to add a different dimension to their music. You might have to soundproof your living room if things get serious ...

BRUSH UP YOUR
CALLIGRAPHY IN CHINA

Duration Four weeks ✳ **Cost** 170 yuan ✳ **Outcome** A meditative mind, an artistic body of work and an understanding of the origin of Chinese, Korean and Japanese script ✳ **Where** Beijing, China

How it suits you

If you're artistic, you'll learn to let yourself be at one with the ink. Self-expression will come as easily as the stroke of a mental brush. Calligraphy has been an important part of China's traditions for centuries; when history buffs are in the capital and see characters carved into a bone inscription dating from 1300 BC, they'll have a deeper appreciation of the skill involved. Inner peace doesn't have to come with inactivity and still meditation. Calligraphy might be perfect for spiritual travellers to actively seek answers within.

What you'll get from it

★ **Relaxation** Painting Chinese calligraphy well requires you to let go of your self-judgement and be lost in the feeling of the process.
★ **Aesthetic appreciation** Chinese characters will no longer be squiggles but a language that can be Rubenesque or statuesque.
★ **Language appreciation** Understanding the relationship between the form and meaning of a character will make you want to learn more. The script you see on your travels will gain meaning, even if it's in the form of 'that looks sort of like Wang'.
★ **Method** As with writing Roman letters, every stroke of every character is drawn in a certain order.

Practical details

The **China Culture Center** (chinaculturecenter.org) in Beijing runs four-week classes throughout the year in English. The classes include meditation techniques, and you can join at any time.

Other options

In the UK, the **Paul Griffiths** (artcourses.co.uk/page/paulgriffiths) art studio runs twice-monthly calligraphy workshops. The **Chinese Culture Center of San Francisco** (c-c-c.org, click on 'classes') conducts seasonal calligraphy courses. In Australia, the **Ku-ring-gai Art Centre** (www.kmc.nsw.gov.au, click on Art and Recreation) in Sydney also conducts Chinese painting and calligraphy classes.

Doing it at home

Now that your characters look strong and healthy, how will you show off your new skills? On greeting cards or letters? Take up Chinese brush painting and highlight your own backyard in a modern take on the calligraphic art form? If you've fallen in love with the Chinese characters, will you try learning the language?

WHAT TO EXPECT

Behold before you what the Chinese call the 'four treasures of the study' of calligraphy or *shufa* – the brush, ink stick, paper and ink stone. The bamboo brush is more than a tool, it's an extension of your arm, your calligraphy master tells you. Today he is gently guiding you through painting Chinese characters as an art form, not as a way to memorise words. Yet the centuries of meaning in each

Free your mind and take a trip to a character-building art class disguised as a language and history lesson.

stroke do linger.

Take the Chinese surname Wang 王 (king). Let the traditional music soothe your body while you grind your ink stick into the ink stone with the perfect balance of water for harmony. Wield your brush vertically and draw three horizontal strokes – one for the heavens above, one for the people below and one for the earth under their feet.

Feel each brushstroke as if you are painting, not writing. Now draw one vertical line to link all three strokes down their centres, brush dancing. This is the character for king, the man who unites the people with heaven and earth.

Your master soothingly encourages you to try again, but to see the ink as the black blood of each character. The brush bristles are bundled from animal hairs, and the Chinese say that your strokes should have bones, sinew and flesh – after all, this art form has been alive here for over 4500 years, since language developed.

Once you have your style, you'll learn to paint on a paper fan or scroll. But for now, breathe and keep letting the *qi* (energy) course from your body through to the brush.

The writing's on the wall ... and the clothes: if you wrote this well you'd probably want to wear it, too.

BUST CAPOEIRA MOVES IN BRAZIL

Duration Two to four weeks ✳ **Cost** R$15 to R$20 per class ✳ **Outcome** Find your abs, bewilder an attacker and gain membership to a growing global tribe ✳ **Where** Salvador da Bahia, Brazil

What's cool about *capoeira* is that no matter how good you get, you can always aim higher.

Variously described as a martial art, a dance form and a secret form of communication amongst African slaves in Brazil, a course in *capoeira* is history in action.

Together with your friendly 'opponent', you step into the circle formed by your peers. Musicians set the rhythm and your *mestre* leads the group in song, the ancient narrative imparting wisdom about life and love. Your opponent fakes you out, then crouches low and springs with a high leg sweep. Feeling a rush, you jump back and cartwheel out of his way before throwing a kick of your own. Welcome to the world of *capoeira*.

If it's all feeling a bit Jackie Chan meets breakdancing meets the samba, no wonder – you're performing an Afro-Brazilian martial art developed right here over 400 years ago by Africans brought to the world's first slave market. Couched in a practice that looked like dance, *capoeira* was used as a form of communication by slaves sold to work on the sugar plantations. Through *capoeira*, they could also defend themselves and attack their oppressors.

With a rich and colourful history (the practice was outlawed), *capoeira* is an increasingly prominent cultural symbol of Brazil and a national sport. You'll find yourself clapping, dancing and singing in an energetic and exhilarating homage to its inventors, as you learn how to do kicks, leg sweeps, rolls and other acrobatic moves. *Capoeira* is ultimately a form of play and a show of skill, so contact is minimal: you'll learn to defend yourself largely through avoidance via some fancy footwork.

How it suits you

Artistic types into colour and movement will want to learn more about the African tribes who started the ball rolling, such as the Yoruba and Bantu. If you're shy and retiring, it's just what the doctor ordered: the music, physicality and strong community feel will shake up your system and bring you out of your shell in ways you never imagined. It's a cinch that social travellers will feel right at home, engaging one to one and studying with a group of international classmates.

What you'll get from it

★ **Self-defence skills** This is a martial art, after all, and – knock on wood you'll never need to use it – you'll learn how to use your body to avoid and block an aggressor, along with a few counter-moves to help keep you safe at home and abroad.

★ **Connection** Connecting with yourself, your circle of peers *(roda)* and those who developed this art form can be unexpectedly and deeply spiritual.

★ **Fitness** The range of movements required will develop your flexibility, balance and coordination. You'll engage muscles you didn't know existed, and ramp up your cardiovascular fitness to boot.

Practical details

For more info about the Salvador da Bahia group, check out **Associação de Capoeira Mestre Bimba** (capoeiramestrebimba.com.br). Instructors may have limited English, but this is easy to get around.

Other options

There are *capoeira* academies worldwide, including Sydney's **Capoeira Academy** (australiacapoeira.com.au), the **London School of Capoeira** (londonschoolofcapoeira.com) and Angolan Capoeira (newyorkcapoeiracenter.com) at the New York Capoeira Center.

Doing it at home

Like yoga, *capoeira* can become a lifelong practice for fitness and spirituality, and there are different styles to try. Find a group nearby so you can work towards becoming a bonafide *capoeirista*. Or sign up for a related activity, such as the samba.

TAP OUT A RHYTHM
DANCING IN IRELAND

Duration One night to three weeks ✳ **Cost** €10 per class ✳ **Outcome** Learn how to reel and jig, get fit and have a craic-ing good time ✳ **Where** Dublin, Ireland

How it suits you

This activity is for the life of the party – step dancing is a fabulous party trick, one to toss out at weddings and down the pub. Besides being a real crowd-pleaser, the active traveller will appreciate the fitness benefits: all that jumping and kicking definitely gets your heart rate racing.

What you'll get from it

★ **Steps** Though improvised dancing at Irish pubs is fun, knowing the actual steps will earn you clout with locals.
★ **Killer calves** Traditional Irish dance requires a whole lot of jumping. Your calves will reflect that, and your quads probably will, too.
★ **Coordination** Practising the steps of a reel or jig will improve your overall coordination and rhythm.
★ **Connection** Irish dance is social and a way to immerse yourself in the craic, whether it's dancing at your lesson or afterwards in a pub.

Practical details

Learn steps through **Set Dancing Lessons** (setdancing. com), a community enterprise that holds classes across Dublin on Tuesday, Wednesday and Thursday evenings throughout the year.

Other options

In the US, Irish dance is alive and kicking thanks to rich Irish heritage and the dance's popularity in the past decade. The **New York Irish Center** (newyorkirishcenter. org) offers adult lessons at all levels. Down under, **Set D@ ncing Australia** (setdancing.com.au) offers beginners' workshops and classes.

Doing it at home

Practise on your kitchen floor, then bust your moves at the next dance party. Irish step dancing never fails to be a crowd-pleaser. If you need a more appropriate opportunity, throw a St Patrick's Day party, or at least hit the bars on this all-things-Irish holiday.

WHAT TO EXPECT

Ireland's traditional dance just happens to be energetic and beginner-friendly, with infectious music that prompts toe-tapping and hand-clapping from onlookers. Though the music alone inspires even lead-footers to jump out of their seats and get hopping, why not learn the proper steps and kicks to impress your friends back home?

Irish dance has earned international recognition through the likes of Lord of

Dance an Irish jig on the Emerald Isle to the tune of a fiddle and the thwack of spoons – and watch out, Riverdance!

the Dance and Riverdance. Though you might be able to watch Irish dance at home or abroad, the Emerald Isle is the place to go to learn it. Here in Dublin, dance is just one manifestation of Irish *craic* (in a word, fun), and so ingrained that you'll see rosy-cheeked pub patrons dancing spontaneous jigs or schoolchildren tapping at high speed in a parade.

Irish dancing comes in two forms: soft and hard shoe. Beginners start in soft shoe, learning the steps of traditional set dances. A gentle immersion course will ensure that the adult beginner feels comfortable, and it's a fun and social setting – no costumes or hairpieces here. Classes are drop-in and held at different locations throughout the week. You'll learn

the steps to basic reels and jigs, and then dance socially for the remainder of the class. The lessons start over every few weeks, so beginners will always feel welcome.

Because the classes are community oriented, you'll find a great mix of locals and foreigners, and you'll leave with a connection to one of Ireland's most colourful and spirited traditions.

Once you've got the basics, try mastering the moves of the Rince Na Chroi Irish dancers, who have jigged across the globe.

Inside the forest *wat* you will find your senses succumb to the serenity.

FIND INNER CALM AT A BUDDHIST RETREAT

Duration 10 days ✳ **Cost** 2000 baht ✳ **Outcome** Smoother temper, honed awareness, and a longer attention span ✳ **Where** Wat Suan Mokkh, southern Thailand

Ever wondered how Thailand gained its reputation as 'The Land of Smiles'? Look to the Buddha. The Thais' indomitable, sunny calm – practically a national characteristic – has a lot to do with the country's long history of Buddhism. A philosophy based on fostering peace, tranquillity and detachment from destructive stress tends to have a healthy effect on your mood.

You can get an insight into Thailand's serene culture – and grab yourself an invigorating dose of mental medicine – by embarking on a 10-day meditation retreat at Wat Suan Mokkh (the name means 'The Garden of Liberation'), a forest monastery in southern Thailand. What you'll mainly be taught, especially for the first section of the retreat, is *anapanasati*, or 'mindfulness with breathing' – in other words, learning to concentrate by focusing on your breath, and letting the tumult of your thoughts come and go unregarded. It's a surprisingly powerful tool.

There are many places around the world where you can learn to practise meditation, but this has got to be one of the most luscious. The monastery is set in hectares of bright green forest, and you'll be doing your deep breathing in a big communal hall that's open at the sides to the trees. And though the rules of the retreat are strict – you must observe silence at all times, rise early, live on two vegetarian meals a day, and abstain from reading, writing, smoking, drinking and sex – the lifestyle can come to seem surprisingly luxurious. There's yoga every morning, walking meditations, chanting in the afternoons and regular dips in the monastery's natural hot springs.

How it suits you

This is obviously one for the spiritual types, those looking to contact a deeper part of themselves and connect with a sense of the oneness of all things. Artistic types will also enjoy the almost hallucinatory ideas and images that surface from the still well of the calmed mind – this could be where your next novel or film is born! Adventurers will enjoy the challenge of adjusting to the retreat's discipline and delving into their internal landscape. And you chaotic types? This is an opportunity to see exactly how many wild monkeys are running the show down there!

What you'll get from it

★ **Wonder** Try watching, say, a crimson dragonfly drink water from a leaf through the prism of your meditation-honed consciousness.

★ **A bit of shush** Not talking to anyone for 10 days can be amazingly refreshing but may ruin you for small talk.

★ **Perspective** Get off the emotional merry-go-round for a while, and then ask yourself – do you need to ride it quite so often?

★ **That Land-of-Smiles Smile** You're breathing calmly, you're detoxed, and your heart's nicely juiced with compassion towards all things. What's easier than a grin?

Practical details

Wat Suan Mokkh (watsuanmokkh-idh.org) is 640km south of Bangkok, near the village of Chaiya. The nearest city is Surat Thani. Retreats start on the first of each month and you need to arrive by 3pm at the latest on the preceding day to register. It's not possible to make reservations – just show up.

Other options

You can do Buddhist meditation retreats in just about every country in the world, including the UK, the USA, Europe, Australia and New Zealand. A good start would be to Google 'vipassana' and your destination of choice.

Doing it at home

Now that you've found the secret of lasting serenity, don't you want to share it and help everyone around you to be as supremely chilled as you are? Why not take a weekly morning meditation at your workplace or with your family?

Get away from the hurly-burly, take a long, deep breath and tame the 'wild monkey' of the mind at a meditation retreat in the Thai jungle.

CONVERSE IN CATALAN IN THE BALEARIC ISLES

Duration 30-hour course ✳ **Cost** €50 to €100 ✳ **Outcome** You'll leave Ibiza with more than just sunburn, a hangover and hazy memories of wild nights out ✳ **Where** Ibiza, Spain

How it suits you

Catalan courses are best suited to the culture-vulture type who is looking for a little bit more from the notoriously party-oriented island of Ibiza. It involves a time commitment to get to classes and do the homework, but your efforts will be doubly rewarded when the hidden layers of history and tradition come alive through the conversations you'll have with the local *Eivissencs*.

What you'll get from it

★ **Dream holiday** It's not hard to have a great time in Ibiza – white-sand beaches, exquisite Spanish cuisine and the world's best DJs pumping out beats in the world's biggest and best clubs.

★ **Sense of belonging** Learn Catalan and make your visit more than just a holiday – instead of just jetting in and jetting out, you'll feel like a part of you belongs on the island, and part of the island belongs to you.

★ **Catalan clout** You'll be able to wow the four million people in Spain and France who are native speakers of Catalan, and who are always ready to share their culture with interested travellers.

Practical details

The regional government heavily subsidises the teaching of Catalan, which means you have access to accredited courses with professional teachers for low prices. Classes for all levels are organised by the **Institut d'Estudis Eivissencs** (estudiseivissencs.cat) and are held year-round.

Other options

Most countries have a small but energetic Catalan community who hold cultural events and conversation classes. Contact Catalans living in Britain through **Catalans UK** (catalansuk.com), or continue your Catalan lessons and follow current events in the US with the **American Institute of Catalan Studies** (aics-usa.org). In Australia, the **Catalan Centre of Victoria** (ccvictoria.cat) holds an excellent annual film festival and has links to all things Catalan.

Doing it at home

Now that you've learnt Catalan you're pretty much an honorary citizen. So next time FC Barcelona make it to the final of the Champions League, get your crew together, grab your flags and some Estrella Damm beer and get loud – *Força Barça!*

WHAT TO EXPECT

As you nervously take your seat like it's the first day of school, you're probably wondering why you're in a classroom when you could be lying on one of Ibiza's famed beaches, working on your tan and planning your next night out cavorting in the island's nightspots. But then you start chatting with Juan Luis or María

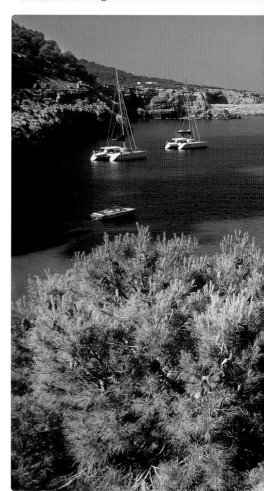

Get involved in the history and culture of the Catalan language against a backdrop of Mediterranean beaches and bouncing mega-clubs – it's what teachers really mean when they say learning can be fun.

Dolores, and they tell you what it's like to live in Ibiza all year-round.

You meet up with classmates during the week to work on your irregular verbs, but you soon find they're inviting you to a bonfire party on an eco-farm or asking if you'd like to come and check out the flower-power fiesta held for the almond harvest. You don't know what that is until you get there, but when you do, you meet people whose ancestors reconquered the island from the invading Moors. They're unable to stop smiling when you ask them, in imperfect but impressive Catalan, which is the best and most secluded beach that none of your friends at the hostel could ever find.

On an island that everyone visits for a good time, not a long time, meeting the locals halfway and speaking their language is a secret handshake that will introduce you to entrancing places you won't find in the guidebooks.

There's more to Ibiza than all-night parties; there are beaches as great as Cala Salada

The stakes are high as you negotiate Island Peak's daunting summit ridge.

EARN YOUR ICE AXES
ON A HIMALAYAN PEAK

Duration From 20 days ✳ **Cost** From US$50 per day ✳ **Outcome** Mountaineering know-how and the self-confidence that can only come from challenging nature and winning ✳ **Where** Nepal

With the possible exception of people with vertigo, who hasn't fantasised about climbing a Himalayan peak?

Sure, you could always go trekking, but having climbed to the shoulder of the Himalaya, it seems a shame not to push for the summit. At US$10,000 per person just for the permit, Everest is probably out of reach, but the 33 summits designated as 'trekking peaks' – a misleading title, as all of these 5650m to 6500m mountains require crampons and ice axes – can be climbed for a much more modest outlay. Even better, Nepali agencies have decades of experience of taking first-timers and transforming them into novice mountaineers in a matter of weeks.

The first step is picking your peak – perennial favourites are Island Peak (6189m) and Mera Peak (6476m), both conveniently close to the trekking route to Everest. Tramping up this famous trail provides vital acclimatisation for the final push from base camp to summit.

En route, you'll learn the ropes (ahem) of Himalayan mountaineering, from essential safety knots to the correct way to arrest an uncontrolled slide. An added perk is the chance to leave the tourist trail and trek through remote villages, where the main sounds you'll hear are yak bells and chanted mantras, rather than the rhythmic clickety-click of trekking poles.

How it suits you

An adventurous nature is pretty much mandatory if you plan to haul yourself up the Himalaya without prior experience of mountaineering! Being able to rely on the best mountain guides in the world will certainly help, but ultimately, the person kicking crampons into the sides of glaciers will be you. In the process, you'll test your limits and experience the thrill that comes from conquering untamed nature.

What you'll get from it

★ **Satisfaction** After gruelling days of trekking and climbing, what could beat the rush of making it to the top?
★ **Training** Mountaineering isn't something you learn in the classroom – this is learning by doing, step by step, knot by knot, hold by hold.
★ **Self-knowledge** Summiting a 6000m peak will reveal all your inner strengths and weaknesses; if you've ever asked yourself 'What am I made of?', this is one way to find out. Wonder Who could fail to be blown away by the view across the roof of the world from the top of a Himalayan peak?

Practical details

Equator Expeditions (equatorexpeditionsnepal.com) is a veteran agency offering guided climbs to the summit of Island and Mera peaks. Find other operators through the **Trekking Agencies Association of Nepal** (taan.org.np). Peak climbing season runs from October to November and February to March.

Other options

Conquer some of the Rockies' most dramatic peaks, with expert help from the **Colorado Mountain School** (totalclimbing.com). Beat Mont Blanc, on a guided summit expedition from Chamonix, or set your sights on the summit of Mt Cook, aided by the able mountaineers at **Alpine Guides** (alpine guides.co.nz).

Doing it at home

If you've developed an appetite for altitude, start the search for fellow mountaineers at your local climbing gym, and train extensively on shorter routes before setting off for your first independent ascent.

Get a taste of how Edmund Hillary felt and learn the art of mountaineering en route to the summit of one of Nepal's lofty 'trekking' peaks.

CLOWN AROUND ON
STAGE IN NEW YORK

Duration 6 days ✳ **Cost** US$800 ✳ **Outcome** A face of a hundred expressions and making anybody laugh without even speaking. ✳ **Where** New York City

How it suits you

Being a clown is for jokers, people with children, people who want to frighten adults, and lovers of the spotlight. It's a chance to let the inner (naughty) kid out and dazzle the world with balloons in the shape of animals – even grownups clap for an animal balloon. Shy types needn't dismiss putting on a pair of floppy shoes – many find the alter-clown-ego a way to bring out an extroverted side they may never have known was in them.

What you'll get from it

★ **Laughter** How can you keep a straight face acting like a kid high on candy? Expect carloads of fun as you discover how silly a pair of braces can make you behave.
★ **Focus** If your head is a big top of emotions, being a clown will teach you to both release and focus those feelings.
★ **Sea change** Let loose the absurd kid in you who you've always wished would come back to give two fingers up to the stuffy adult world.

Practical details

NY Goofs' Clown School runs classes throughout the year for beginners or actors. Graduates can apply for their stage performances. See nygoofs.com for details.

Other options

Clown courses are plentiful all over the USA and Europe. Search for schools at nosetonose.info or clown-school.com. If you want to get serious and love a black-and-white stripey top, visit the Marcel Marceau Paris International School of Mimodrama (as in mime) at mime.info/EIMP_help.html

Doing it at home

Hold on to your bow tie, there's more to do than just be on stage. Entertain sick kids in hospital (laughter cures all) or scrap your suit for dungarees and start a party clown business. And even if you never paint your eyes white again, you'll still have the lifelong skill of being able to make people chuckle by screwing up your face.

WHAT TO EXPECT

Welcome to New York City, home of Broadway. Show me excited. Now sad. Quick, give me puzzled. Work it, clown. Whether you're on stage or at a kid's party, being an adult in white makeup is not just about 'honk-honk' but also the high-energy of improv.

There's nothing like a mask to let out the huge, manic smiles inside you. Or that heart-breaking pout. Your clown persona

Plonk on a bulbous red nose, curly wig and plastic flower to make kids giggle while scaring the socks off adults.

is constructed from your inner feelings and natural inclinations of voice, movement and gesture. This school lets you play like a child again, learning to be spontaneous through theatre games and physical comedy tricks. Let yourself be completely britches-splittingly ridiculous. Think Bozo, Krusty (from New York, by the way) or Marcel Marceau – all lovers of the absurd.

Some come to clown school to learn how to make sick kids in hospital guffaw, how to persuade New York's tourists to drop coins into their floppy hats, or to become versatile actors. But everybody starts with that tub of white face grease as they learn to paint in a new person. Once you get your clown on, you'll learn how to show your personality without even

uttering a word – through classes on comedy, costume and learning to move like a cartoon character.

Students have gone on to perform with the Ringling Bros and Cirque du Soleil, so this is no laughing matter (tee hee). In Russia, clowns study for years and are revered the same way as ballerinas or pianists are.

Big fun under the big top: circus skills raise a smile.

GRADUATE FROM GELATO
UNI IN BOLOGNA

Duration Two weeks ✸ **Cost** €1500 ✸ **Outcome** Gelato-making skills, inspired taste buds and the key to a food-lover's heart ✸ **Where** Bologna, Italy

As part of your research, you'll need to sample the goods from every *gelateria* you pass. Alas!

Crazy for gelato? Pump up the passion factor and smooth your way to a cool new career by learning to make this famous frozen treat in the culinary heart of Italy.

WHAT TO EXPECT

Feel the joy from the moment you alight from your Vespa and feast your eyes on buckets filled with creamy milk, sparkling sugar, brilliantly coloured berries, succulent fruit and chocolate chunks. After mastering the art of gelato, you may never eat mere ice cream again.

Hear the word gelato and your mind conjures up sunny vacation days, cobblestone streets and a delightful ending to a robust Italian meal. Here in northern Italy, a region that accounts for more than half of the nation's consumption of this delectable dessert, you'll take your place in the 'university' lecture hall in front of the *maestros* who really know their stuff.

Usual classroom expectations melt away as your animated instructor hands out delicious samples and begins an operatic instruction in the art and science of gelato-making. Lesson one: it contains less air and less fat than American-style ice cream.

Soon you're rolling up your sleeves in the workshop, where you're the alchemist, choosing and hand-blending ingredients and learning how to use machines that swirl and freeze your creation.

It seems like child's play, but the pros are soon separated from the amateurs in this class – you'll learn to calibrate the creamy goodness so it's not too heavy or too light, too buttery or sandy. Along the way, your instructors will train your taste buds and inspire ideas for recipes, plus teach business fundamentals for your own gelataria – a growing enterprise across the globe.

How it suits you

Detail-oriented travellers will love learning all the ins and outs and formulas needed to succeed in the world of gelato. Once the basics are mastered, artistic cooks will be able to let their creativity run rampant with the invention of exotic new flavours that could put them on the map.

What you'll get from it

★ **Method** Everyone's obsessed with 'balance' these days and here we're talking fat versus sugar: you'll learn how to get that combination right for the correct consistency, aesthetic value and maximum flavour hit.

★ **Culinary creativity** With so many potential ingredients to choose from, there are endless combinations to try. This is risk-taking at its best – will that be basil, blueberry merlot or parmigiano gelato today?

★ **Passion** Let's just say it's an osmotic process as you learn directly from Italians who have chosen the creation of sweet, happiness-inducing food as their life's work.

Practical details

Carpigiani Gelato University (CGU; gelatouniversity.com) is a 20-minute drive from the centre of Bologna. Courses run year-round. CGU recommends accommodation options – and even sells gelato-making machines.

Other options

CGU offers courses around the world: check the website. In the UK, try a short course in artisanal ice-cream making at the **School of Artisan Food** (schoolofartisanfood.org). In Australia, **Pure Gelato** (puregelato.com.au) offers an evening gelato appreciation course in Melbourne, while the **Gelato and Pastry Institute of America** (gpiamerica.org) runs courses in Ronkonkoma, New York.

Doing it at home

Where was your sweet spot? Immersion in Italian food culture or the joy of creating a delectable dessert? Check out the availability of local gelatarias (extensive tasting required!) and work on a business plan to take it all the way. Or keep the Italian passion burning with a cooking or language class.

PRACTISE SILK PAINTING IN NEPAL

Duration As long as you need ✳ **Cost** By donation ✳ **Outcome** Insights into an ancient artform, phenomenal skill with a brush and a sense of inner peace ✳ **Where** Kathmandu Valley, Nepal

Not a still life: Durbar Square in Kathmandu.

Embark on an artistic journey that blends brushwork and meditation like paint on a palette by learning the ancient art of silk painting from a Kathmandu lama.

WHAT TO EXPECT

Think about the ground rules of modern art – no boundaries, no restrictions and anything goes. Now imagine the polar opposite. In *thangka* painting, every sweep of the brush has a profound meaning, forged over thousands of years of Buddhist teaching. Before you make your first brushstroke on stretched silk, you'll need to learn the lexicon of Tibetan Buddhist art: the dharma wheel, the eight lucky signs, the seven precious jewels – and a who's who of deities, saints and gurus.

Don't expect to master this intricate painting style overnight. Students in Nepal's *thangka* schools study for years to learn the ritual and science of *thangka* painting, as well as the technique.

Step one is to establish the grid that defines the proportions for the painting – think Da Vinci's *Vitruvian Man* but a hundred times more complicated. Only when you've cracked this intricate geometry can you begin to populate your painting with enlightened beings and auspicious symbols, and imbue your artwork with meaning.

Guided by a master painter who is part tutor, part spiritual guide, you'll move forward in incremental steps, for this is a journey in which process is as important as the finished artwork. The setting will most likely be a brick-walled house on a narrow lane; your tutor could be a red-robed refugee lama or a jeans-wearing rock fan, trained since childhood in the elaborate art of *thangka*-painting. Either way, you'll learn as much about the psyche of modern Nepal as you will about paint and brushstrokes.

How it suits you

Artistic and spiritual travellers will naturally be drawn to this ancient, sacred art. It takes commitment and dedication to acquire the knowledge and skill to create a perfect *thangka* – some artists devote a year to creating a single piece. If you don't have this kind of discipline, it may be better to stick to admiring the work of local masters in Buddhist monasteries.

What you'll get from it

★ **Understanding** Every *thangka* tells a story – learn the meaning behind the symbols and you'll be able to read Buddhist art like a scripture.
★ **Precision** There's no room for slapdash workmanship here; make every brushstroke a perfect spiritual statement.
★ **Patience** Preparing the grid for your *thangka* is just the first step – it takes dedication to paint intricate detail into every inch of the canvas.
★ **Knowledge** If nothing else, you'll learn enough about Tibetan Buddhism to start putting all the gurus and bodhisattvas into context.

Practical details

Any of the *thangka* schools in Kathmandu, Patan and Bhaktapur can put you in contact with a master teacher. Try **Lama Thangka Art Center** (thangkapaintings.com) in Thamel, which is experienced in arranging painting courses for foreign students.

Other options

For more cross-cultural artistry, study dot painting with Aboriginal teachers on a painting course at the **Janbal Gallery** (janbalgallery.com.au) in Mossman, Queensland. Finish each stroke with a flourish on a Chinese calligraphy course at the **Hong Kong Art School** (hkas.edu.hk), or acquire the archaic art of icon-painting at an Orthodox monastery in Russia.

Doing it at home

The raw materials for *thangka* painting are easy to find, but the hard part is finding the right points of reference. Buddhist study will point you in the right direction; enquire about courses at local Tibetan Buddhist organisations.

DIVE FOR PIRATE BOOTY IN THE CARIBBEAN

Duration A few days to a few weeks ✳ **Cost** US$300 for an Open Water course ✳ **Outcome** A pirate accent, a deep tan and the Caribbean's best-value dive licence ✳ **Where** Utila, Honduras' Bay Islands

How it suits you

if you're an intrepid adventurer, the challenge presented by endless underwater beauty – not to mention pirate booty – will be irresistible. If you like the idea of winding down to a semicoma, Utila's sandy, car-free streets, fruity cocktails and plentiful hammocks will do the trick. And if you're a pirate, you'll feel right at home.

What you'll get from it

★ **Cheap thrills** You'll get more dive practice for your buck here than just about anywhere.
★ **Big chills** It's hard to imagine a more laid-back people than the Utilans, and it won't take long for you to catch on.
★ **Arrrrrgh!** You'll be talking like a pirate within days.
★ **Good fun** As a mecca for dive-happy budget travellers, Utila's bar scene and night life are as colourful as its pirate legends.

Practical details

Utila is just a short boat ride off the coast of Honduras at La Ceiba. Once there, choose from countless dive schools. For an overview, see the **About Utila** (aboututila.com) website.

Other options

The world is dotted with beautiful dive sites, but you won't find too many as laid-back and inexpensive as Utila. Nha Trang in Vietnam comes close – try **Deep Blue Diving** (vietnam-diving.com) for recreational dives.

Doing it at home

Unless you live in some landlocked hell-hole, your new PADI or NAUI licence will be valid to dive anywhere there's water. Dive in!

WHAT TO EXPECT

Join divers from around the world who come to the Honduras Bay Island of Utila to earn their dive licences on the cheap, before descending to the depths in search of Captain Morgan's lost treasure.

In the 17th century, Utila was a pirates' paradise. English, French and Dutch pirates, including Welsh buccaneer Henry Morgan, laid hideouts all over the Bay Islands, perfect for launching raids on

Plunge into a pirate's lair in the underwater world of Utila, one of the Caribbean islands dotting Honduras Bay.

Spanish vessels laden with bullion bound for Europe. By the mid-17th century there were some 5000 pirates hidden away in their island lairs.

Today, though part of Honduras, Utila's natives speak English, and their culture remains filled with pirate lore. Pirate descendants stroll the sandy streets, greeting each other with Caribbean buccaneer accents that would make Johnny Depp swoon.

Pirate treasure still lies deep beneath the waves, so no wonder the island's main attractions are underwater. There are myriad dive schools to choose from – take your pick and go snorkelling with whale sharks and dolphins, or develop your dive skills with an Advanced Open Water course.

And if you can't stand all that ear-popping and tank-wearing, Utila offers endless alternatives. Go kayaking around the Utila Cays, stopping to snorkel, picnic and soak up some vitamin D on the coral beaches. Hike up Pumpkin Hill to check out some pirate lairs or just hang out in a hammock with a glass of Captain Morgan's rum at a seaside bar.

Even if you don't find treasure in Utila, your new dive skills will give you access to majestic reefs in every ocean.

MAKE YOUR OWN
MOSAIC IN RAVENNA

Duration One week to one month ✳ **Cost** From €550 ✳ **Outcome** Art and history appreciation, hands-on restoration know-how and plenty of Gaudí techniques ✳ **Where** Ravenna, Italy

Look up for inspiration: mosaics, such as the majestic interior dome of St Apollinare's, are everywhere in Ravenna.

> **Step back in time in the former capital of the Western Roman Empire, where monumental Early Christian mosaics light up dark Byzantine churches.**

If you're a lover of mosaics, you've no doubt already heard of Ravenna's shimmering mosaics of Sant'Apollinare, San Vitale and Galla Placidia. These glittering mosaics mark the highpoint of the art form in medieval Europe, so if you've never seen them, you're in for a treat.

Between the fall of the Roman Empire and the advent of the High Middle Ages, Ravenna's fortunate citizens were enjoying a protracted golden age while the rest of the continent flailed in the wake of Barbarian invasions.

Ravenna's gold shines no brighter than in the city's famous Unesco-listed mosaics, sparkling emerald and sapphire masterpieces that embellish half a dozen terracotta-bricked 4th- to 6th-century churches and leave most visitors struggling for adjectives. A suitably impressed Dante once described them as a 'symphony of colour' and spent the last few years of his life admiring them. Romantic toff Lord Byron added further weight when he spent a couple of years here before decamping to Greece.

Those not content to wax lyrical with the aesthetes can pursue a more proactive vacation, as a handful of local mosaic schools set up by skilled Italian artists and restorers in the 1940s and '50s can help you mimic, re-create and – should you be suitably up to it – restore these amazing works of art. The top organisations are run by experienced mosaic artists and offer courses of between one to four weeks – that's plenty of time to immerse yourself in this surprisingly un-touristed Italian city with those who know it best.

How it suits you

Mosaic making will appeal to artists, or wannabe artists, who love history and have the desire and diligence to master a notoriously intricate art form. A creative mind helps, as do meticulous technical skills, and you'll need to be anally retentive enough to cope with the painstaking details. Italophiles will enjoy the magnificent setting in the quintessential Italian region of Emilia-Romagna, famous for its gastronomy and grand palaces.

What you'll get from it

★ **Attention to detail** There are no short cuts in placing tiny pieces of coloured glass and stone into intricate patterns – mosaic artists are patient and meticulous beings.

★ **Historical insight** Immersing yourself in Ravenna will awaken you to a splendid but little documented chapter of history: the final flourishing of the Western Roman Empire on the European continent.

★ **Artistic vision** The Early Christian mosaicists were true visionaries; their work provides some of the most striking and unique examples of the genre in the world. Any attempt to emulate their methods will send your own artistic vision rocketing into the stratosphere.

Practical details

There are numerous mosaic schools in Ravenna and they are perennially popular with foreign visitors. Reputable multilingual organisers include **Gruppo Mosaicisti** (gruppomosaicisti.com) and the **Mosaic Art School** (mosaicschool.com).

Other options

Mosaic courses are widespread: in the UK **Mosaic Matters** (mosaicmatters.co.uk) collates information. American mosaic artist **Sonia King** (mosaicworks.com) organises annual workshops in Istanbul, one-time capital of the Byzantine Empire and another important font of Early Christian mosaics.

Doing it at home

After your Ravenna trip, you may hatch a plan to redo your patio or retile your fireplace. An ability to lay out intricate mosaics is a plus for those diving into DIY or interior design.

CHILL OUT WITH TAI CHI
IN HONG KONG

Duration One hour, three times a week ✳ **Cost** Free ✳ **Outcome** Grace, patience and a cultural understanding of slow-mo moves ✳ **Where** Hong Kong, China

How it suits you

Tai chi will appeal to spiritual types as it's considered much more than physical exercise. It's a mental and physical healing mechanism, a type of meditation and a soft form of martial arts. It's also a philosophy, the continuous and smooth 'forms' representing the unity of yin and yang in life. If you live in a chaotic environment, this is your escape route, as it is for many Hong Kongers.

What you'll get from it

★ **Basics** This isn't a degree in Sinology; you'll learn the basic tai chi concepts and recognise why so many Chinese are into the activity.
★ **Cultural insights** To understand tai chi is to understand a centuries-old art form, and you'll be one step in that direction.
★ **Amusement** There's a smile behind the seriousness. Finding yourself in an odd pose with a group of strangers is a fun way to start the day in a foreign country.

Practical details

The **Hong Kong Tourist Board** (discoverhongkong. com) runs hour-long tai chi classes from 8am on Monday, Wednesday and Friday at the Hong Kong Museum of Art in Kowloon. The classes are part of the board's Meet the People cultural program, which includes Chinese cake making, tea appreciation, Chinese opera appreciation, architecture walks and feng shui classes.

Other options

In Australia, Sydney's **Lane Cove Tourist Park** (lanecoverivertouristpark.com.au) runs free tai chi lessons. In the US, New York's **Greenbelt Nature Centre** (nycgovparks.org) on Staten Island runs tai chi classes every Sunday. There are plenty of courses online to help you mug up before your next trip to China.

Doing it at home

Once you're hooked on tai chi, you'll notice it's more popular at home than you figured. Most big cities have tai chi centres and societies, or try scouting around your local Chinese community for free sessions in parks and gardens.

WHAT TO EXPECT

William Ng might look like a little old Cantonese man, but his strength belies his stature. His white satin *changsan* glimmering in the morning sunlight, he commands the utmost respect. Ng and his accomplice Pandora Wu are your qualified instructors, with a brief to make tai chi more accessible to Hong

Unite the mental, physical and spiritual elements of movement on your first step to enlightenment, health and general yin-yang equilibrium.

Kong's growing number of overseas visitors. And so they do.

First up, Ng deftly demonstrates how to 'hold the ball', 'grasp the bird's tail' and do the 'single whip'. It's an unhurried, seamless sequence of poses, like kung fu in fluid slow motion, and without the cartoon sound effects. Ng makes

it look mesmerisingly easy, but then it's your turn. Think of it as learning the 'Lawnmower' or the 'Sprinkler', except this isn't a disco dance floor – it's a tree-studded courtyard in Kowloon, one of the few open spaces in one of the most densely packed cities in the world. An audience can be expected.

Never fear, you won't be the only one putting your tai chi moves out there. Known as the 'art of awareness', tai chi is practised religiously by young and, more often, old in parks and public spaces throughout Hong Kong, mostly in the mornings. Pretty soon you'll be blending in with the crowd.

Tai chi masters say the more you practise, the more self-aware you become.

WORK WONDERS IN WAX
IN INDONESIA

Duration One to five days ✳ **Cost** From 485,000 rupiah per day ✳ **Outcome** An unashamedly psychedelic artwork for your wall or your wardrobe ✳ **Where** Ubud, Bali, Indonesia

Appreciate the scintillating designs in Bali's ubiquitous batik by learning the skills behind them.

Create an alternative work of art infused with your exotic surrounds: paddy-field greens, clear-sky blues and fresh-fruit yellows and pinks.

WHAT TO EXPECT

It's odd, painting with wax. Years of pen and pencil wielding will make a *tjanting* – the tool used to draw with the molten substance – feel quite unusual. But the results can be spectacular.

Batik is an old Javanese word meaning 'to dot'. And where better to try the textile technique of applying dye-resistant wax to cloth to create bold designs than Ubud, Bali's cultural hub. Here, you can let your artistry run riot among paddy fields and Balinese dancers, fuelled by some of the tastiest food in Indonesia (well, it's essential to feed your creativity ...).

One of the best teachers hereabouts studied in Yogyakarta, Java's capital of culture and the home of batik. He brought his unique take on traditional textile design back to beautiful Ubud. Under the tutelage of Nyoman Suradnya you'll learn the history of batik, as well as wax-working, cracking and hand-dyeing tips.

What you paint is up to you. Back in the 12th century, batik was reserved for royals; their favoured patterns were often flowery. Today you can experiment. Perhaps be inspired by your surrounds, which are lush, arty, colourful and carnivalesque – there's always a festival happening around here somewhere.

So, as the inland island heat gathers in your classroom, channel the tropics onto your white-cloth canvas and let your imagination run free.

How it suits you

While making batik is not strictly a spiritual activity (although the rise of Islam did influence its traditional motifs), the more contemplative traveller will revel in the quiet concentration required. Of course, artistic types are well catered for on this mission, but more detail-focused souls might enjoy the technical slant to batik: there are tools and methods to master. That said, one person's wax mistake (an anal-retentive's disaster!) could be another's modern art.

What you'll get from it

★ Creativity What you draw is up to you. Fill that blank cloth with all the sounds and sensations of Bali. Or batik a picture of your mum.
★ Inspiration Learning a new art form from a master practitioner, with a group of other keen souls, promotes the sharing of ideas (or means you can steal other people's ...).
★ Time out Stop being a tourist, start being a local: stay put for several days, spending each day at your easel, and you get what makes Indonesia tick.
★ Pleasure What's not to love about playing with paint and hot wax?

Practical details

Nyoman Suradnya (nirvanaku.com) runs one- to five-day batik courses at Nirvana Pension in Ubud. Lessons include tips on dip-dyeing and *tjanting* techniques, and all students will produce their own piece of batik.

Other options

Drag yourself off the beaches around Krabi, Thailand, for batik workshops, cultural activities and homestays at Baan Nateen traditional village. Or enrol on a three-session batik course at Kuala Lumpur's **Malaysian Institute of Art** (mia.edu.my).

Doing it at home

Batik isn't as convenient as simple sketching – there's more *stuff* involved. That's not to say you can't continue, however. How about hosting a big batik bash, especially if you've just moved house. Invite a group of friends round, order in some wax, protect your table tops and get your mates to make you a unique set of scatter cushions.

PLAY FOLK MUSIC IN NORTH CAROLINA

Duration Week or weekend courses ✳ **Cost** US$320 to $620 ✳ **Outcome** Bluegrass rhythms, mountain culture and your own handmade dulcimer ✳ **Where** Brasstown, North Carolina, US

If you'd like more twang in your step and bluegrass in your repertoire, North Carolina's Blue Mountains is where old-school Appalachia lives on.

WHAT TO EXPECT

Up here in the Blue Mountains of North Carolina, it's easy to feel folky. Trying your hand at quilt-making, wood-turning or blacksmithing – or, better yet, becoming a bluegrass master by taking a make-your-own dulcimer class.

The John C. Campbell Folk School is a feel-good, mingle-with-new-people place that gives a real break from (much of) the modern world. (No TVs! Bearded locals!) If you come alone, you won't stay that way. You start the day by singing a 'morning song' with the group, then dine with your classmates at communal tables. Plus most of the rooms are in 1920s historic farmhouses.

'It's a really relaxed environment,' says school staffer Keather Weideman. 'Once you're here, you grasp it. Travel can be better when you spend a week learning something.'

Founded in 1925, the school has a rustic vibe and fills a lush setting in a Blue Mountain valley riddled with hiking trails. Each week, all year-round, visitors come to attend one of 16 immersion classes that bring out the joy of 'traditional mountain culture' – everything from banjo, woodcarving and quilting, and making a mountain dulcimer – an Appalachian creation – that they'll then teach you how to play.

How It suits you

If you're a people person, this is a very social setting – you will end up exchanging email addresses (even if you're not checking email while here). If you're artistic, you can take advanced courses, but most classes are suited for those with no art skills. If you're details-oriented and like to feel organised, much of the day is structured around learning a task.

What you'll get out of it

★ **Americana** Pick an old-school slice of Americana, and learn the skills so you can do it yourself at home.
★ **Musicality** Combine construction with lessons, and take home your very own mountain dulcimer.
★ **Gooey** Everyone goes soft at these classes, joining up as a team and learning traditional skills.

Practical details

The **John C. Campbell Folk School** (folkschool.org) runs classes year-round, with week immersions and weekend classes. Brasstown is about two hours from Atlanta, Georgia.

Other options

You can take fiddle, mandolin and banjo classes at Brooklyn's **Jalopy** (jalopy.biz) in New York. Colorado's popular **RockyGrass Academy** (bluegrass.com) is a family-oriented, open-air workshop held every July in Lyons, while the **Old Time Music and Dulcimer Festival** (oldpalmusic.com) is held in March in Palestine, Texas. Or go all out at **East Tennessee University** (estu.edu), the world's only four-year school with a bluegrass music studies department.

Doing it at home

It's easy to bring a slice of Appalachia home. Surprise your uncle on his next visit by pulling out your mountain dulcimer. Then hop online and see what the **Friends of the Mountain Dulcimer** (mountaindulcimer.ning.com) are up to.

Prepping your dulcimer is
hard graft but you'll be rewarded
with dulcet sounds for decades.

CLIMB ANCIENT TREES
IN OREGON

Duration Daytime or overnight ✳ **Cost** From US$200 ✳ **Outcome** Experience life in the tree-tops, climb tall trees safely, and learn how to pee into a bottle ✳ **Where** Central-west Oregon, US

The only way is up: get to grips with Oregon's tall, green trees.

Re-create memories of your 10-year-old self by scaling giant trees in the dense rainforests of the Pacific Northwest.

WHAT TO EXPECT

It stands to reason that Eugene, a city that helped popularise tree-sitting as a means of environmental protest in the 1990s, would be equally expert in the art of tree climbing. Based out of one of the US's most environmentally congruous cities, Eugene's professional tree-climbers will have you climbing into the canopy of an old-growth rainforest in no time.

Sandwiched in between the Cascade Mountains and the Pacific coast, Eugene sits on the cusp of some of the finest and most accessible forest in the contiguous US. Nearby is the prized Willamette National Forest, a haven of hemlock, cedar and fir trees flecked with a thousand different shades of green.

Launched by a couple of sport-climbing arborists in the early 2000s, the Pacific Tree Climbing Institute offers day and overnight trips to the abundant Oregon forests where you can shin up an old-growth Sitka spruce or Douglas fir for the ultimate tree climb. If the primate in you still isn't satisfied, the institute gives you the opportunity to spend the night amid the leafy branches in a specially rigged hammock.

The trips are designed to be challenging and fun but there's a strong element of ecotourism in the experience. Embrace the notion that these ancient leafy behemoths, many of which are older than Europe's medieval castles, are a precious commodity that exist to be cherished (and climbed!) rather than logged.

How it suits you

Tree-climbing is considered an esoteric and 'extreme' hobby by some, so no wonder it attracts a blend of adventurers, fresh-air fiends, greenies, nature lovers and climbers in search of a break from the rock face. You'll need to be more whimsical than the average mountaineer to enjoy hanging out above the ground in a dense forest canopy. The ability to 'rough it' is also a prerequisite. Overnight climbers stuck up a tree for 12 hours can't be fussy about bathrooms; peeing into a bottle is one of the spin-off skills.

What you'll get from it

★ **Head for heights** Vertigo sufferers will beat their fear of heights and find that the Zen-like adventurism of hoisting yourself up into the high branches outweighs the fright of looking down.

★ **Appreciation of nature** If you're not already a tree-hugger you might well become one after this vertical hike into the ethereal world enjoyed by birds, insects and the odd scurrying squirrel.

★ **Climbing skills** Climbing adeptness isn't purely confined to craggy rock faces and frozen waterfalls. Scaling towering old-growth trees fed by several century's worth of heavy rain takes a fair amount of skill, know-how and specialised equipment.

Practical details

The **Pacific Climbing Institute** (pacifictreeclimbing.com) is your best option for a safe, organised excursion, and they're flexible with times and locations. Rain is a given in this part of the world, especially between October and April, so summer is the best time to go climb a tree.

Other options

Tree Climbers International (treeclimbing.com) is a group of people who love climbing trees, based in Atlanta, Georgia. Down under, **Tree Climbers Australia** (treeclimbers.com.au) hosts courses and climbs in and around Brisbane, Queensland. The 2011 International Tree Climbing Championship (ITCC) is an annual opportunity to garner tree-climbing inspiration.

Doing it at home

Practise in the park with your kids and relive childhood memories, or pursue a career as an arborist. Walks in the woods with a much greater appreciation for your leafy surroundings.

PERFECT ITALIAN PIZZA
ON THE AMALFI COAST

Duration Five days ✳ **Cost** €567 ✳ **Outcome** Neapolitan pizza recipes, techniques for cooking pizza in your oven, nonstop requests for homemade pizza ✳ **Where** Sant'Agnello di Sorrento, Italy

How it suits you

If you're the type of person who enjoys meeting new people, this family-run school will appeal to you as it's a very genial, sociable atmosphere, and teaching is frequently in groups. If you like to go with the flow, you'll enjoy the spontaneous feel of being welcomed into an Italian family for a few days. The opportunity to explore the beautiful Amalfi Coast between cooking lessons will keep adventurous types fired up.

What you'll get from it

★ **Confidence** You'll learn how to perform every stage of the pizza-making process, gaining a surprisingly simple, yet impressive, culinary skill.
★ **Delight** Eating a pizza in Campania is a delectable experience, and even more so with the satisfaction of knowing you made it yourself.
★ **Passion** To cook excellent pizza, it needs to be done with some Italian ardour.
★ **Relaxation** There'll be plenty of time to unwind, eat, explore and sit in the sun between the lessons, but cooking can be a relaxing process in itself.

Practical details

The **Mami Camilla** (mamicamilla.com) cooking school is in Sant'Agnello di Sorrento, 50km south of Naples, around an hour away by train or bus. The school is open year-round, with classes running for two hours daily, Monday to Friday.

Other options

Learn the traditional art of Italian pizza with **Enrica Rocca** (enricarocca.com), who has schools in both London and Venice. Her London courses involve a visit to Borough or Portobello market to source ingredients. Native New Yorker Mark Bello teaches hands-on artisanal pizza-making classes at his **Pizza a Casa** (pizzaacasa.com) school in New York.

Doing it at home

Once you've learned how to make Neapolitan pizza in a conventional oven, you can experiment. You'll have learned the traditional toppings, but you can try out different flavours and combinations to create your own variations on the classic meal-on-the-go.

WHAT TO EXPECT

Put Naples' reputation for pizza primacy to the test: is Neapolitan pizza the best in the world? You'll find out firsthand and learn how to get hands-on with pizza dough at this family-run cookery class on the gorgeous Amalfi Coast.

Whether pizza originated in the Naples region is a matter of dispute, but most food experts agree that the people of Campania were the first to try a tomato topping on

Learn to cook the world's best pizza in the sun-dappled surrounds of a family-run cooking school — and re-create the taste of an Italian summer in a flash.

their base, after the introduction of this strange fruit by the Spanish in the 16th century(the word for tomato, pomodoro, means 'apple of gold').

Mami Camilla's is a family-run cooking school in a Sorrento suburb on the Amalfi Coast, an suitably pretty place to learn this most delectably simple of dishes. The school is housed in a whitewashed building, a former olive oil factory,

surrounded by lemon trees. Lessons are taught by Camilla's husband, Biagio Longo, in the high-ceilinged kitchen, hung with copper pots.

Usually pizza is wood-fired at 500°C, way hotter than conventional ovens can reach. The school teaches traditional techniques but you can also learn how to make good pizza in your oven at home, just in case you don't have a brick-built pizza oven

tucked away in your garden.

You'll also be taught how to prepare the dough and shape it by rolling it over the back of your hand. Taste the different traditional toppings used in Neapolitan kitchens, learn how to create the optimum tomato paste, and find out how to ensure you'll achieve a perfectly crisp crust – every time. You'll never order takeaway pizza again!

Between lessons, take time to admire the pretty Amalfi coastline.

DANCE THE TANGO IN BUENOS AIRES

Duration As long as it takes ✹ **Cost** From AR$100 ✹ **Outcome** Learn a whole new language, become a night owl and understand the porteño soul ✹ **Where** Buenos Aires, Argentina

It takes two: learn the language of tango in Buenos Aires.

Learn how to sashay like a seasoned *tanguero* in Buenos Aires, where the sexy tango was born.

WHAT TO EXPECT

Learn how to dance like a tango diva in Buenos Aires, and you'll join a fascinating nocturnal subculture. Many a tango novice has found the dance devilishly addictive – before long, you'll be out all night, sleeping all day and living the authentic *porteño* lifestyle.

At once both sultry and melancholy, the tango is the 'embrace that is danced', the unstoppable pulse of the city of Buenos Aires. The tango's intimacy and beauty are part of BA's character, and essential to its soul.

The tango's history began in the bars and brothels of the city's colourful port area, La Boca. Here, immigrants from all over Europe mingled their own musical traditions with local rhythms like *candombe*, which arrived a century or so earlier on African slave ships. The rhythm and lyrics combined to symbolise the plaintive cry of the homesick immigrant, the jilted lover's bitter lament and the *porteño's* hymn to Buenos Aires.

Like many cultural touchstones – samba in Brazil, clogs in Holland and beach pedicures in Bali – tango can at times be in your face and clichéd, but behind the bevy of bedazzled dancers posing for photo opportunities in San Telmo and La Boca, there's a rich cultural legacy to discover. Away from the public displays and dinner shows there are *milongas* (tango dance halls) across the city, from cavernous ballrooms to intimate clubs, their dance floors packed with tangoing couples. Strap on your high heels and discover it takes far more than two to tango in BA.

How it suits you

Tango welcomes all – the morbidly depressed, the sexually exuberant, the cocaine-addicted, the recently out-of-jail. Find a translation of the lyrics, and you'll learn that it's a dance for misfits, lovers and good-for-nothings alike. Emotional types with a tendency veering towards the dramatic will feel an immediate affinity with the passionate strains of the bandoneón and the overwrought lyrics of tango's songs.

What you'll get from it

★ **Porteño soul** Listen and be moved – heard in Buenos Aires' bars, taxis and dance halls, tango is the story of Buenos Aires' history and people.
★ **Etiquette** You'll soon learn the intricate rituals of the *milonga* – a subtle nod or glance is all you need to find a partner and hit the floor.
★ **New footwear** Never was there a better excuse to spend up big on elegant high-heeled shoes in countless hues.

Practical details

First of all, you need the footwear. Luckily, tango shoe stores are also the best places to pick up the latest tango news and to talk to other *tangueros* about the best places to dance and study. Try **Comme il Faut** (commeilfaut.com.ar) for shoes, the **Escuela Argentina de Tango** (eatango.org) for classes and **BA Milongas** (buenosairesmilongas.com, in Spanish) for up-to-date *milonga* listings.

Other options

The international tango craze started in late belle époque Paris – check out **Le Temps du Tango** (letempsdutango.com) for lessons in the city that took the tango to its heart. You can also learn to tango at any number of schools throughout the world, from Brisbane to Tokyo.

Doing it at home

Just as there are schools the world over, so too are there *milongas* everywhere. A quick online search should quickly put you in touch with your local tango scene. Online shoe supplier **Greta Flora** (gretaflora.com) can get your feet into gear, and to keep up your music supply, check out **Zivals** (zivals.com).

Steve Raymer / National Geographic Society / Corbis ©

INDEX

INDEX

COOKS, CLOWNS AND COWBOYS

101 SKILLS AND EXPERIENCES TO DISCOVER ON YOUR TRAVELS

PUBLISHING DIRECTOR Piers Pickard

PUBLISHER Ben Handicott

COMMISSIONING EDITOR Errol Hunt

ART DIRECTION & DESIGN Mark Adams

LAYOUT DESIGNER Frank Deim

EDITORS Janet Austin, Mardi O'Connor, Sophie Splatt

IMAGE RESEARCHERS Rebecca Skinner, Claire Gibson, Barbara Di Castro

PRE-PRESS PRODUCTION Ryan Evans

PRINT PRODUCTION Larissa Frost

WRITTEN BY Andrew Bain; Robin Barton; Sarah Baxter; Mark Beales; Sarah Bennett; Joe Bindloss; Abigail Blasi; Catherine Bodry; Claire Boobbyer; Celeste Brash; Janine Eberle; Jane Egginton; Ethan Gelber; Sarah Gilbert; Tienlon Ho; Jess Lee; Shawn Low; Rose Mulready; Robert Reid; Simon Richmond; Daniel Robinson; Sam Rutter; Brendan Sainsbury; Craig Scutt; Regis St Louis; Matt Swaine; Phillip Tang; Caroline Veldhuis; Lake Waterson; Penny Watson

THANKS TO Robin Barton, Liz Abbot, Sasha Baskett, Nicholas Colicchia, Helvi Cranfield, Karina Dea, Bruce Evans, Chris Girdler, Jane Hart, Bronwyn Hicks, Trent Holden, Carol Jackson, Charity McKinnon, James Phirman, Kirsten Rawlings, Sue Stone, Nicole Trevan.

Published in December 2012 by
Lonely Planet Publications Pty Ltd
ABN 36 005 607 983
90 Maribyrnong St, Footscray,
Victoria, 3011, Australia
www.lonelyplanet.com

ISBN 9781743210215

© Lonely Planet 2012

© Photographers as indicated 2012

Opening image - Thai Elephant Conservation Center, Lampang, Thailand; Felix Hug / Getty Images

Printed in China

LONELY PLANET OFFICES

Australia

90 Maribyrnong St, Footscray, Victoria, 3011
Email talk2us@lonelyplanet.com.au

USA

150 Linden St, Oakland, CA 94607
Email info@lonelyplanet.com

United Kingdom

Media Centre, 201 Wood Lane, London, W12 7TQ
Email go@lonelyplanet.co.uk